GLOBAL
SOCCER
MOM

CHANGING
THE WORLD
is EASIER THAN
YOU THINK

GLOBAL SOCCER MOM

SHAYNE MOORE

ZONDERVAN.com/
AUTHORTRACKER
follow your favorite authors

For my children—
John David, Greta, and Thomas

ZONDERVAN

Global Soccer Mom
Copyright © 2011 by Shayne Moore

This title is also available as a Zondervan ebook.
Visit www.zondervan.com/ebooks.

This title is also available in a Zondervan audio edition.
Visit www.zondervan.fm.

Requests for information should be addressed to:
Zondervan, *Grand Rapids, Michigan* 49530

Library of Congress Cataloging-in-Publication Data

Shayne, Moore. 1970-
    Global soccer mom: how I learned I could change the world / Shayne Moore.
      p. cm.
    ISBN 978-0-310-32558-1 (softcover)
    1. Mothers—Religious life. 2. Church and social problems. 3. Women in
church work. 4. Moore, Shayne, 1970- I. Title.
    BV4529.18. M662—2010
    253.085'2—dc22   2010009041

Published in association with the literary agency of Alive Communications, Inc., 7680 Goddard Street, Suite 200, Colorado Springs, CO 80920. www.alivecommunications.com

Cover design: *Studio Gearbox*
Cover photography: *Michael Hudson Photography, Veer*®
Interior design: *Michelle Espinoza*

Printed in the United States of America

10 11 12 13 14 15 /DCI/ 22 21 20 19 18 17 16 15 14 13 12 11 10 9 8 7 6 5 4 3 2 1

CONTENTS

It starts with you. In the end, God simply calls you to be faithful to the things He has given you to do. He doesn't require you to be a superstar, just faithful and obedient.

World Vision President Richard Stearns,
The Hole in Our Gospel

This is what compassion means. It is not a bending toward the under-privileged from a privileged position; it is not a reaching out from on high to those who are less fortunate below; it is not a gesture of sympathy or pity for those who fail to make it in the upward pull. On the contrary, compassion means going directly to those people and places where suffering is most acute and building a home there.... It is the compassion of God who does not merely act as a servant, but who expresses the divinity of God through servanthood.

Henri Nouwen, Compassion

FOREWORD

"The Office of the President? Yeah ... right." My assistant smirked and hung up the phone.

"Who was that?" I asked as I picked up a stack of receipts off of her desk and headed to mine to sign them. She joined me, answering, "Hmmmphh. Some guy claiming he was with the Office of the President."

"The president of what?" I asked.

"The United States."

"As in George Bush?" I queried. "Seriously?"

"Yeah, sales people will try anything." She turned back toward her desk to pick up the ringing phone. Curious, I followed and saw her shocked face, her eyebrows raised. *"Really?* This *really is* the Office of the President?"

Three days later I walked up some steps to the White House to join nineteen other leaders of the evangelical world for the President's Briefing on HIV/AIDS. There were only three women: Beth Moore and Anne Graham Lotz and ... me. I had no idea why I'd been included. Sure, I was the CEO of an international outreach to moms of preschool-age children — hundreds of thousands of them — but why me?

For eight hours I listened to briefings, discussions, and finally a press conference in the East Room. The highlight? Honestly, it was a few minutes in the Blue Room when I talked Max Lucado into calling our office back in Denver and cheering on our staff. *Max Lucado!*

While I left with my head spinning over the startling and devastating statistics of the disease and a new word in my vocabulary—*pandemic*—I couldn't see what my role in righting this wrong might be. I couldn't change the world.

A decade and another administration later, God dead-ended me into a passage in the gospel of Mark (14:1–9) where I discovered a story that changed my life. Jesus received Mary's gift of nard and responded, "She did what she could." These five words grabbed me and haven't let go. I don't have to do it *all* to make a difference. I simply need to act. To put feet on my faith. I can make a difference in the everyday—whether noticed or not. Agreeing to dogsit my son's Rottweiler. Taking time for coffee with a stressed-out mom. Sponsoring education and relief for a child in a Third-World country. Voting. Reading this book and letting its story stir me to *care* and then to *do something*.

When I *do what I can* ... I can change the world.

And so can you.

Yep, you. Just a regular woman. A working woman. A make-it-on-your-own single woman. A wife. A mom. Even a soccer mom.

Shayne Moore is just such a mom. Going about her days as busy mom in the fast lane of kids and husband and home, she bumped headlong into the heartbreak of HIV/AIDS and poverty and ... well ... *human need*. Stunned with the size of the struggle compared with her apparent inconsequential offering, Shayne recoiled. That is until she discovered that the only path out of the trauma around her took her step-by-step into an everyday compassion . . . moving her to simple actions that impact our world.

Read on. Take in the journey of a woman *just like me—just like you*—who took first one step and then another to do what she could and is now changing her world. Follow the nudge of Jesus in your heart and discover what you can do. Change your world.

Elisa Morgan,
October 2010, Publisher, *FullFill*™, www.fullfill.org,
Speaker, Author, *She Did What She Could*

A PRAYER

Almighty and eternal God:
May your grace enkindle in all of us
a love for the many unfortunate people
whom poverty and misery
reduce to a condition of life
unworthy of human beings.

Arouse in the hearts
of those who call you Father
a hunger and thirst for social justice
and for fraternal charity
in deeds and in truth.

Grant, O Lord,
peace in our days,
peace to souls,
peace to families,
peace to our country,
and peace among nations.
Amen.

Pope Pius XII

WHO AM I TO MAKE A DIFFERENCE?

An Introduction

> I want to explore justice. I use this word as shorthand for the intention of God, expressed from Genesis to Revelation, to set the whole world right—a plan gloriously fulfilled in Jesus Christ, supremely in his resurrection, and now to be implemented in the world. We cannot get off the hook of present responsibility by declaring that the world is currently in such a mess and there's nothing that can be done about it until the Lord returns.
>
> *N. T. Wright,* Surprised by Hope

> We ourselves feel that what we are doing is just a drop in the ocean. But the ocean would be less because of that missing drop.
>
> *Mother Teresa*

I am an ordinary full-time mother of three. I don't think of myself as a feminist, per se, or a liberal, or a member of the religious right. I'm a housewife, mother, lover, and friend. I start most days by throwing on my go-to pair of jeans and pulling my hair into a ponytail. My calendar is full of school events, sports practices, and instrument lessons. I holler at my kids to pile into the car as I rush to cram in one more load of laundry—and never mind the unfolded clothes on the table. It is my job to make sure everyone has clean clothes, good food, and homework papers that are turned in on time.

This book is for women like me—ordinary women who want to make our world a better place. Even though I now spend most of my life in the car shuttling kids from one activity to the next, there is much more to me than that—and I suspect there is much more to you as well.

In the political world, the term "social justice" is often used to describe the activities of working to eradicate injustices such as poverty and disease. In our churches we use the word *missions* or *missional*. Historically, mission departments in churches were about spreading the gospel message and conversion, with a smaller focus on meeting the physical real-life needs of people around the world. In fact, in the conservative faith tradition I grew up in, "social justice" and "activism" are scary terms used to describe liberals. However, when I consider that 16,000 children die every day from malnutrition and extreme poverty, or that more than 1 billion people live on less than $2 a day, social justice no longer sounds like a secular or church issue, conservative or liberal issue. When I consider that gender-based violence against women and girls is pervasive in the developing world and that women and girls are marginalized and exploited in situations of extreme poverty, advocating or speaking up on their behalf no longer looks like a Democrat or Republican issue. It seems to me to be a compassion issue.

There is much division in the world today, both in the political arena and in the church. In my Protestant tradition, we disagree on things such as women's roles in leadership, what to do with the homosexuality issue, and the style of worship music. It can be confusing and use up a lot of our time and energy as we debate the minutia of Christian life. I may never have all the answers when it comes to what divides the church or our nation; however, if I am sure of one thing it is this: I am not wrong if I am spending myself on behalf of the poor and the oppressed.

In our churches we pray the Lord's Prayer every Sunday and we say, "Thy kingdom come, Thy will be done [on] earth, as it is in heaven" (Matt. 6:9–10 KJV). I am confident extreme poverty, the exploitation of women and children, and preventable diseases are not in heaven. I can act in this world, in my time, to fight these things, knowing I am in the will of God.

The book of Isaiah (58:6–11), says it this way:

> *Is not this the kind of fasting [or expression of faith] I have chosen:*

> *to loose the chains of injustice*
> > *and untie the cords of the yoke,*
> *to set the oppressed free*
> > *and break every yoke?*
> *Is it not to share your food with the hungry*
> > *and to provide the poor wanderer with shelter—*
> *when you see the naked, to clothe him,*
> > *and not to turn away from your own flesh and blood?*
>
> *[If you do these things . . .]*
>
> *Then your light will break forth like the dawn,*
> > *and your healing will quickly appear;*
> *then your righteousness will go before you,*
> > *and the glory of the LORD will be your rear guard. . . .*
> *If you do away . . . with the pointing finger and malicious*
> > *talk,*
> *and if you spend yourselves in behalf of the hungry*
> > *and satisfy the needs of the oppressed,*
> *then your light will rise in the darkness,*
> > *and your night will become like the noonday.*
> *The LORD will guide you always.*

I am a full-time mother with a busy life, and that is not going to change anytime soon. Even if I never move to Africa, become a missionary, or march on Washington, can my heart still break for what breaks God's? Do the boundaries of my life keep me from making a difference?

Do the boundaries of yours?

My journey began in my hometown, but it's taken me to Africa and Honduras and to international economic summits. I have met high-profile activists like Bono and George Clooney and worked with African activists like Ugandan nurse Agnes Nyamayarwo. I have stood shoulder to shoulder with prominent Republicans and Democrats on Capitol Hill to testify that issues of global poverty and disease need not divide us.

In fact, they ought to unite us.

What will your journey look like? What ministry or issue will God place on the path of your life? As ordinary moms, can we become compassionate global thinkers? Can we raise our voices against what breaks our hearts?

I used to believe that my life and my family's lifestyle stood in opposition to working on behalf of social justice ideas and advocacy. I felt I was a sellout because my family and I live in a comfortable suburb and we attend a status quo church. I wondered if I had become a part of the problem. This was a thought that nagged at me, and I stuffed it down deep for years.

Our world is changing. Not all of us are called to huge activities outside our house, our town, our church — but all of us are called to do something. We have unprecedented access to each other, to ideas, and to resources. Even as moms, we can come to the global table and join the conversation; even our "ordinary" lives affect the life and death of real people around the world. In fact, the feminine voice has been absent from this table for too long. Women are the caretakers of the world, and we *must* have a say.

But let's back up a few steps. I'm not a policy expert, and I never will be. I'm not a preacher or a politician. I'm simply a mom who is learning to follow God's call to fight injustice and suffering in my world. When I started my journey, I did not have models or guides on how an ordinary woman from Middle America could get involved with global need. I knew very little of international policy on anything. Despite stumbling blindly forward, I found guides for the journey in some unlikely people. We all have unique stories, and we all begin our journeys in our own places.

So where are we? Are we in the PTA meetings, the MOPS groups, and the carpool lane? Are we making coffee for Wednesday morning Bible study? Are we at Bible Study Fellowship and Sunday night service? Are we stuck at home with three little kids and barely make it to church at all? Are we professional women and full-time moms who feel we have no extra time for anything? Are we compassionate women of faith who have yet to find a church home? Are we struggling with faith and disillusioned with church altogether?

Wherever we find ourselves by God's creative grace, I believe we're all called to the same goal of making a difference.

Let me tell you my story.

1

CARETAKERS
OF THE WORLD

Women and mothers care for their children and their families — we are the caretakers of the world. When someone is dying of AIDS in Africa, it is a woman who is by the bedside; a mother, a sister, an aunt, a grandmother, a daughter.

Princess Kasune Zulu

The social justice tradition (the compassionate life) is not a set of pious exercises for the devout, but a trumpet call to a freely gathered people who seek the total transformation of persons, institutions, and societies. We are to combine suffering love with courageous action. ... We are to become the voice of the voiceless, pleading their causes in the halls of power and privilege.

Richard Foster, Devotional Classics

LITIEN, KENYA, 2005

The relentless rain pours down. Nothing here is built on level ground. Brown, dirty foam forms where the water is pooling in the waiting area outside the hospital. If the building was once level, perhaps over time this assault of rain has eaten away at the dilapidated hospital and surrounding compounds.

Today I am observing a Kenyan nurse named Nettie, fluent in English, Swahili, and Kipsigis. I attentively stay one step behind, hoping to learn, yet self-consciously trying to stay out of her way. Nettie moves slowly around the waiting area with her clipboard, writing down names and speaking to the many people who braved the storm. She helps an elderly woman find a seat, answering endless questions and laughing with the Kipsigis grandmothers and their grandchildren.

I am not a health-care worker, a missionary, or a government agent. I am fluent in exactly one language. I am a stay-at-home mother with three young children who is in Africa with my church. The African Inland Mission is building a new hospital in rural Kenya, and a team of us from my church are here to do some light carpentry, paint, and learn about the local HIV and AIDS programs.

It has been three years since I first heard of the devastating effects of the HIV and AIDS global pandemic. It has been three years since I first grappled with the statistics: 5,000 children die every day from severe diarrhea; 72 million children (56 percent of whom are girls) remain out of school around the world; every day in Africa 4,400 people die from AIDS; and more than 12 million African children have lost one or both parents to AIDS.

Now the statistics have faces and names.

I silently follow Nettie as I marvel at the earlobes on the Kipsigis grandmothers. Nettie catches me mid-gawk. She explains that the tradition of stretching out women's earlobes was abandoned several generations ago, but can still be seen on older women. Some of the women are dressed in traditional Kipsigis tribal attire, and their ears are so stretched that the circle of flesh reaches down to their shoulders. Nettie chats with them, and I greet them the best I can. We grab hands and smile.

The people look to be on the verge of falling apart, with their rotting and missing teeth, the growths on their faces, the discolorations of the whites of their eyes, and tattered scarves wrapped around alarmingly thin bodies. The absence of consistent medical care is evident at a glance.

Most have traveled a long way to this rural hospital. Cars are scarce and bicycles can be found on the difficult roads, but most people walk everywhere. They come with a variety of ailments — a four-year-old boy with a donkey bite, a five-year-old with a snake bite, a little girl named Daisy with a horrible case of malaria.

Some have come to the Volunteer Counseling and Testing Center (VCT) to be tested for the HIV virus. These clinics are supported by the Kenyan government to encourage people to find out their HIV status. This hospital is staffed by nine counselors, all women, who serve this community.

Nettie explains, "Knowing your status is the first step in arresting the spread of HIV and AIDS. Most of my patients are men, as women fear finding out their status because they will be turned out and shunned by their husbands and families and separated from their children."

She tells me this without emotion, but my brain and heart are having a hard time processing it. This is not the first time I have heard the immensely troubling double standard for men and women regarding HIV and AIDS.

I am a woman from America, and my paradigm for the role of women in society is Western, modernized, and egalitarian. I am trying very hard not to be ethnocentric as I reflect on what I am being told about women, HIV, AIDS, and extreme poverty in Africa. I want to respect the culture and traditions of other people, but this doesn't feel right.

If knowing your status is the first step to arresting the spread of HIV, and women aren't tested, how will the disease be stopped? If a man brings HIV into his home due to infidelity (brothels are common in rural Africa, and men often contract HIV from sleeping with prostitutes), then gives it to his wife and children, how is it okay *in any culture* for that man to throw out his HIV-positive wife?

From Nettie I learned that in this part of rural Kenya, girls are often sexually active at the age of twelve and boys at eighteen. Within the VCT's client base, more men come in for testing, yet more women are HIV positive. Partly this is a result of how a woman is made; she is physiologically more susceptible to contracting the HIV virus.

Nettie also confirms the horrible stories of rape on very young girls, telling me that in western Kasum, an area outside of where we are in Litien, the nurses and home-based caregivers report frequent cases of rape because men believe that sleeping with a virgin will heal them of HIV.

I had traveled the day before with Nettie to Cheborgei, a village forty-five minutes away, where the hospital and community have a home-care group. We are in Kenya during the rainy season, and although the sky is clear, the roads are outrageously bumpy from earlier downpours. The red clay roads seem more like drainage ditches, and we are jostled and jerked in the back of the truck as we wind around the tea fields to the old mission church where the villagers gather.

Upon arrival, my body feels bruised, and I untangle myself from the cramped rear of a 1950s enclosed pickup truck. Nettie and I are greeted by a group of men. The chief of the village is contagiously exuberant. His loud voice booms across the lawn of the church, "God is great! There is no one like our God. We! Are! Happy!"

Tears prick my eyes at the unexpected joyful greeting—and this for an AIDS education meeting. The happy handshakes, greetings, and smiles are extended all around.

An old mission church stands at the center of the small village. The homes have dirt floors, and the walls and roofs are made of sticks lashed together with rope. The church is the only modern structure, and it looks frozen in the 1940s. I half expect to see a white missionary come around the corner dressed up like that lady in the movie *Out of Africa*. It appears the missionaries who built the church and educated this small community have since moved on, but they left behind yellowed posters of Jesus and his disciples, a pile of mildewed hymnals, and an old wooden cross.

Yet this place is alive. Newly planted flowers color the path to the front door. The floor is swept, and the smell of fresh chai tea fills the sanctuary. A bright, clean tablecloth is on the altar. The villagers smile and chat together. The women are talking about something with great passion, and I wish I could understand what one woman seems to be explaining to the others.

About fifty men and women have gathered to hear Nettie teach about HIV and AIDS: how it is transmitted, how to avoid infection, how to practice family planning, and how to avoid infecting children. Once inside the church, the men and women separate themselves, with the men seated on the right and the women on the left.

As a former junior high teacher, I observe that Nettie is a skilled teacher. She has an easy, yet authoritative, rapport with the villagers. She is stern, direct, gentle, and subtle all at the same time. Nettie flows effortlessly between three languages of English, Swahili, and Kipsigis, and as she speaks, her eyes glow with tangible warmth and power. Nettie is a mother of four, and her community calls her "the mother of all." She and I are both thirty-five.

Standing at the pulpit, Nettie asks, "We talked of this last time. Can someone tell me how HIV is spread?"

"HIV is spread through sexual intercourse and needles," a man volunteers from the male side of the church.

As Nettie continues her questioning, most people seem to know the textbook answers. I do wonder about the probability of needles being a problem, as it seems just finding a container to carry water is difficult in this far-flung place.

"I have another question for you," Nettie says. "What do you do if your wife is HIV positive and you are not?"

The church is quiet while people shift uncomfortably in their pews. Nettie looks to the women with hopes of engaging a response from the female side of the church.

No one speaks.

Finally a man says matter-of-factly in broken English, "If your woman, your wife, has got the HIV, you leave that wife behind and marry another."

Nettie is very composed—this answer does not surprise her. But me? It takes everything in me not to fly out of my pew and tackle this man. I want to stand on the altar and scream, "No! No! No!" Instead, I hold back burning tears and try to control my breathing.

At the pulpit, Nettie is composed and, without missing a beat, she directs the same question to the women. "What do you do if your husband is HIV positive and you are not?" Several women indicate a willingness to abstain from sex. I wait, confidently hopeful one of the ladies will push back on what the man said.

Instead, the room is painfully silent. An older woman finally speaks. "If you are married and you cannot ..." She giggles as she cannot seem to say the word *sex* in mixed company. Several uncomfortable chuckles follow. "I mean, if you don't have *that*, what do you have? All you have is cooking and eating."

Everyone laughs as the painful truth is solidified through the safety of comic relief and shared experience. I watch Nettie, who persists, "What do you do if both of you are HIV positive? Do you have a baby?"

With the nodding of heads and murmurs, the room unanimously seems to say, "Of course."

Nettie sensitively points out, "I'm not telling you not to have a baby, but the baby will be infected, and now you have more trouble in your house."

This sad exchange is pushing down on my shoulders and my soul. I drop my head to hide my tears and notice a tattered Bible being held tightly by the woman sitting next to me. I glance up at her to see an ancient and lovely face. The wrinkles etched into her ebony skin tell a tale of a long and beautiful life—how old she is. Her beauty catches me mid-breath, and I almost make a noise trying to breathe again. How old is her Bible? Was it her mother's? Her grandmother's? The cover is ragged and the pages are crumpled and yellow.

I am surprised by how much her act—bringing her Bible to this meeting—moves me. She is far past childbearing years. This strange new virus has brought death to her village and new reasons to gather in her place of worship. A lifetime ago, had she watched this church being built, when strangers brought a new message to her people? Did she once walk to church holding her mother's hand while clutching this treasured Bible in the other?

I do not dare lift my head again as I try to hold in my tears. I keep staring at the Bible and at the ancient feminine hands holding it. They are my lifeline to sanity, or at least cultural appropriateness. Her hands—strong, callused, feminine hands—are keeping me from collapsing on the floor or jumping up to organize the women into some kind of rebellion.

At this church, in this village, the statistics have names and faces.

●

Today at the VTC, we have moved under the lean-to waiting area, and Nettie is shouting to be heard over the rain. I position my feet between two puddles, hoping to stay dry as I listen to the deafening noise of the rain on the tin roof. The woman Nettie is helping seems to be about my age, and a small boy clings to her side. I look down at him, making eye contact, and smile. He looks at me with huge brown eyes, unsmiling, before looking away and pushing into his mother.

Nettie hands the mother a piece of paper. Taking her son by the hand, she walks over to the cutout hole in the plywood wall, to the hospital pharmacy. I see her get some medication and hurry into the rain. I watch her leave, clutching the medication to her chest.

"Nettie, what did you give her?" I ask. "Medication for HIV?"

"Yes." Nettie nods. "She got her ARVs today. She has enough now for this month."

Antiretrovirals (ARVs) are used to treat retroviruses like HIV. Only 3 percent of Africans have access to these life-saving medications, and their availability in rural Kenya surprises me.

I am excited and hopeful. "Where did they come from?"

"The medications came from the government. Every

VCT is allotted a certain amount of ARVs, depending on their need and if they meet the set criteria," Nettie patiently explains.

"They came from the government? Where did the government get them?" I am still fascinated because I have been told not even governments have good access to these medications.

"The government and the pharmaceutical companies they work with recently received a large grant from America. PEPFAR money. Do you know what that is?" Nettie asks.

I let out a quick, surprised sigh. I know about PEPFAR because I lobbied for it. I joined the ONE Campaign, the Campaign to Make Poverty History, in 2003, as Congress and President George W. Bush created the President's Emergency Plan for AIDS Relief. The ONE Campaign and its members called Congress and the White House to urge the passage of this bill, which was signed into law in 2005.

I freeze as I watch the mother and her son disappear down the road. How can I feel such a sense of solidarity and difference at the same time? We are both mothers, but I have rights and options in my culture that she may never have. I have access to medications and a pharmacy around the corner. Without PEPFAR money to provide her lifesaving medications, this mother might live only another year and die while her child is still young. With medications, she might live twenty years. She might raise her child. Work. Go to church. Have a life.

Before urging my government to pass PEPFAR, I had never lobbied my elected leaders about anything. Lobbying was what special-interest groups like the National Rifle Association (NRA) did, not the job of soccer moms.

Now it rains down on me.

In the muddy yard outside the hospital, all the dots are connecting. Stunned, I take in the breathtaking reality that my advocacy efforts, my lobbying, *did something.* Me, a stay-at-home American mother, lobbied for the interests of a Kenyan mother struggling to survive. From the other side of the world, *I helped her.* My few actions are giving this mother a chance to stay alive and care for her child.

Voice for the voiceless.

- As of 2008, Americans have supported AIDS treatment for more than 2.1 million men, women, and children living with HIV/AIDS through PEPFAR.[1]
- Before PEPFAR, only 50,000 people were receiving treatment for HIV/AIDS in sub-Saharan Africa.[2]
- Two pills a day, that cost about 40 cents, can keep someone with HIV and AIDS alive and healthy.[3]
- In sub-Saharan Africa, 4,100 people die daily from preventable, treatable diseases.[4]

SHAKING THE FOUNDATION

The name of this infinite and inexhaustible depth and ground of all being is God. That depth is what the word God means. And if that word has not much meaning for you, translate it, and speak of the depths of your life, of the source of your being, of your ultimate concern, of what you take seriously without any reservation.... He who knows about depth knows about God.

Paul Tillich, The Shaking of the Foundations

Here we are touching the profound spiritual truth that service is an expression of the search for God and not just of the desire to bring about individual or social change.

Henri Nouwen, Compassion:
A Reflection on the Christian Life

Illinois, 2002

Today is a crisp, bright autumn day, the kind of October moment the Midwest produces when on its best behavior. There is energy in the sunlight as it laces the crimson leaves. I turn my car onto the hospital campus run by local Franciscan Sisters. The electric yellow oak trees are showing off their autumn wardrobe. The statues of Mary, the Holy Family, and St. Francis catch my attention as I wind my car under the fall canopy to park. Although I did not grow up Catholic, I have always been drawn to these depictions of ancient men and women.

As I walk toward the entrance of the hospital, I notice a convent belonging to the Franciscan Sisters next door. I stop to pick up a perfect leaf—half orange and half crimson—to give to my sick friend. Stan is a friend from college who was struck down with Guillain-Barré syndrome, a muscular and neurological disease. He has come to Marion Joy Rehabilitation Center to recover. It has been a scary time for our whole community. Living in my hometown, I am blessed to do life with many dear friends. Stan's sudden illness sent a shock through all of us.

My visit ends as Stan is wheeled to a physical therapy session. I walk soberly down the halls of the rehabilitation center. I look up and, seeing a small cross indicating the hospital chapel, I feel compelled to enter and pray. Alone, I kneel in the quiet and plead to God for healing and mercy on behalf of my friend and his family.

I sometimes hear God speaking to me. Some people have asked, "How do you know you're not talking to yourself?" I don't have an answer other than, "I just know." As I kneel and pray for Stan, God keeps telling me to go next door to the convent. "I am in here to pray for Stan," I say out loud, piously reminding God about what's really important.

Go. Go.

Getting off my knees, I mutter, "Fine. I'm going."

I follow the white sidewalk to the convent and enter glass doors that lead me to a breezeway. Reaching for the next set of doors, I pull hard — only to almost hurt myself tugging on locked doors. I let out a humored sigh and look around. To my right, I see a large black button and above it a sign, "Buzz for admittance."

Buzz. Buzz. I chuckle to myself and stare through the locked doors, taking in the contents of the lobby. It is extremely white — white tile, white walls, and white plastic furniture. There are statues and pictures of Mary and St. Francis. There are, however, no people who can unlock these doors.

I shake my head and say out loud, "What am I doing here?"

Except that I know with knowledge beyond myself that I am in the right place. God is under me and behind me, practically pushing me to this door. I stand, fidgeting back and forth, for about a minute.

Finally I hear footsteps from behind and turn to see a

sister dressed in regular street clothes coming to open the glass doors. She is lovely, with short brunette hair, a round face, and a big smile. She reaches for the lock with her keys in hand, opens the door to the lobby, and gestures for me to enter, asking, "Is there something I can help you with?"

I follow her into the bright lobby. Her face and eyes look at me as though she is delighted to see an old friend. Wherever this is going, I am sure she is coming with me. Since I do not know the reason for this divine errand, I blurt out a question about mentoring.

"Well ..." she responds, "what exactly do you mean by mentoring?"

Quickly making conversation, I say, "Years ago a friend told me the sisters here might offer spiritual guidance."

"Oh," she says, smiling, "you're looking for a spiritual director. Here, sit down." She points to a couch covered in plastic. "Tell me about yourself."

I go with the moment and summarize a lifetime of my religious experience, complete with the joys and frustrations that accompanied it. She smiles and seems pleased with my story and my reason for loitering in her breezeway. She asks if I know anything of St. Francis.

"My friend Juleen just called me the other night to relay a story she had just read about St. Francis," I say, finding this coincidence rather providential.

"This is the story of Francis's conversion," I say. "Francis hated lepers and was scared of them. He despised their begging and the bugs that crawled all over them. One day while riding his horse, he saw a leper begging and yelling. He was repulsed, but he suddenly felt a compulsion to get off his horse and go to the leper. The leper's face was a huge disgusting sore. Francis took the leper's hand and kissed the rotting flesh and the wounds."

I am feeling good about recalling the story so well, and the Sister is still smiling encouragingly, so I continue. "Then the leper suddenly disappeared and Francis began to sing. The story explains how Francis embraced what he feared. He learned to understand and cherish each individual as a unique reflection of God's creative genius, and a true attitude of compassion began to form within him."

We are smiling at each other. The nun brings her hands together in a clap of pleasure. "You know the story!" She adds excitedly, "The revelation of Francis is all people *are* Christ! We are to see past the created, the individual, and see the Creator."

We are instantly bonded, and I want to hug this Sister in her cheap pumps and navy skirt.

"I haven't introduced myself," she says warmly. "My name is Sister Gabrielle."

My knowledge of St. Francis earns me a tour of the convent, and Sister Gabrielle asks if I would like to see their chapel. I am honored to receive the invitation to see the intimate space where the sisters interact with God, and I quickly agree. We walk down a long tiled corridor and pass a table with a display on our right.

I stop and stare. "What is this?"

"This is our Center for Peace, Justice, and Integrity of Creation," she says.

All the nerve endings in my soul start firing at the same time. I had never heard of a Center for Peace, Justice, and

Integrity of Creation. What do they do there? My world, my church, and my life do not include such a place. My heart pounds as a voice from the depth of me says distinctly, *"This is what pleases me. This is what it's about."*

Gabrielle moves me along, seeming not to notice the expression on my face or my teary eyes. "Today is a day of contemplation and prayer, so the sisters have spent the whole day in here." She opens the double glass doors that lead into the chapel.

About twenty elderly sisters are sitting in silence on pews throughout the room. To my great pleasure, in the center aisle is a fountain. The only sound in the room is the gentle trickle of water.

Light pouring from the ceiling draws my eyes up, and I gaze at the expansive stained glass window spanning the room 360 degrees. "It's beautiful."

"It's Mary's Magnificat. Are you familiar with it?" Gabrielle asks. Then, in a whisper, "My soul glorifies the Lord and my spirit rejoices in God my Savior, for he has been mindful of the humble state of his servant." As she recites, she gestures with her arms, joyfully displaying the windows to me.

I put my hands to my heart. "I do know it. It's beautiful," I say wistfully. Then I confide, "My church meets in a high school gym."

We return to the hallway and, when we no longer have to whisper, she says, "If you have time, I would love to show you our cosmic statue of St. Francis out on the grounds."

Cosmic is such a powerful word to communicate great expanse and mystery, and it is not a word often used in my conservative faith tradition. I almost grab her as I enthusi-astically say, "It makes me so happy you just used the word *cosmic*! I would *love* to see the statue!"

Sister Gabrielle and I step out into the sunlight and the conversation flows.

"I've grown up in this town," I say, "but I have to admit I know very little about the Franciscan Sisters."

"The Franciscan Sisters started in Germany in 1866," Gabrielle responds.

I listen attentively as I am now thoroughly convinced I heard the voice of God with clarity when I was told to go to the convent. I do not want to miss one thing he wishes to show me.

She continues, "We began with four young women who accepted the challenge to serve the poor, sick, and aging in their village. From this small group grew the Franciscan Sisters of the Sacred Heart."

We turn down a paved path and cross a large yard. "From the early years, the sisters spent long hours serving those in physical and spiritual need. They cared for the sick in their homes, nursed victims of smallpox and typhoid fever. They taught the young and opened the convent to orphans and the elderly. Eventually, around 1920, they left Germany and settled in Indiana. Over time, the Sisters moved here to Illinois."

I nod, keeping step with my new friend. "How are the Franciscan Sisters connected with St. Francis?"

"St. Francis calls us to a life of peace and respect for creation. He calls us to simplicity and poverty. Our culture is drowning in individualism."

I nod as if to say, "I see your point, but I'm a bit uncomfortable with it."

Gabrielle goes on, "Francis tells us to abandon our lives in complete obedience to something bigger than ourselves. We strive to have profound gratitude and humility toward God, our world. Oh, and to the flawed institutions that have nurtured us." She waves her hand toward the convent as if to communicate her understanding that the church will never be perfect.

The nerve endings in my soul are firing again. My eyes are burning, holding back tears. These ideas have lured me before. I took a vow of poverty once. Serving God and having a heart for the poor and engaging with those in need was a lifestyle I once embraced to the point that I lived and worked in the inner city. But I got married. I left the city, and that time in my life seems foggy and distant.

Gabrielle stops mid-path. "Our campus consists of sixty acres and holds a home for HIV-positive patients." She points to the long white building I saw driving in. "Look behind you and you can see the tops of the low-income housing we offer to the community."

I recognize the buildings. They are across the street from Target. Suddenly, I am painfully aware that I have passed those buildings hundreds of times, wishing they were nicer, worried about who lived in them, or at least wished them to be farther off the road so I didn't have to see the porches piled with toys and clothes drying on a makeshift clothesline.

"We also run a hospital, a rehabilitation center, and a convent. We host various events in the community as well. We recently had a Peace Walk. It was a great success!"

I am staring at her, trying to hold all the thoughts rushing at me. Gabrielle touches my arm to indicate we ought to keep moving down the path.

We pass through a line of trees, crunching the leaves under our feet, and emerge on an open field. On the far side of the meadow, I see a dark figure in the midst of exploding sunlight. Gabrielle and I approach in silence. St. Francis stands with his arms outstretched to heaven. He is clothed in his traditional robe with an amber halo of stained glass crowning his head. In his right hand he raises up a crescent moon and five stars. In his left hand he holds the solar system — a twisted sculpture of stained glass and metal depicting the sun and the planets. The sunlight pours through the stained glass, sending off prisms of light.

The bronze St. Francis is mounted on a platform representing the earth. Surrounding him and carved in the base are images: a snake, a hawk, birds, leaves, trees, and a deer. Engraved around the base of this cosmic statue a nun had penned a poem:

May Francis remind us that all creation, whether above or below, is ...

... sister and brother.

Gabrielle and I stand in silence. I let the cosmic statue draw me in. I am utterly grounded. As I gaze at the sunlit statue, I hear the silent, thunderous voice of God saying over and over, *"This is what pleases me ..."*

3

VOICES

In the world to come I shall not be asked, "Why were you not more like Moses?" I shall be asked, "Why were you not more like Zusya?"

Rabbi Zusya, early Hasidic leader and folk hero

Beneath the noise
Below the din
I hear your voice
It's whispering
In science and in medicine
"I was a stranger
You took me in."

U2, "Miracle Drug"

WHEATON, ILLINOIS, 2002

I smile sweetly to my youngest child. "Thomas, are you thirsty? Here ya go."

Thomas giggles, takes the sippy cup, and promptly throws it on the floor. The phone rings. I am thankful for a distraction from this project.

"Shayne! Bono is coming to Wheaton College!" Juleen yells into the phone the minute I answer.

"What are you talking about?" I ask as I pick up the cup for the tenth time. I have been trying to get my one-year-old to transition from the bottle to a sippy cup, and it is not going well.

"Listen to me. Bono is doing a tour to raise awareness of AIDS in Africa, and I just found out he's coming to speak at Wheaton. Today."

"What?" I leap off my chair and gesture madly with my hands. "This is crazy. Is he speaking in chapel?" I glance at the clock. "Oh, no! Chapel starts in ten minutes." I holler to my four-year-old, "Greta, get your shoes on!"

"Are you going right now?" Juleen is laughing.

Unlatching the high chair tray and grabbing Thomas, I say, "I'm leaving! Meet me there!"

My mind races as I drive my minivan the few blocks which separate my home from my alma mater. Juleen and I attended Wheaton College, a small Christian liberal arts college, and I can't help but be somewhat in shock as I wonder, *How can this be? Since when does Wheaton College give rock stars a platform to speak?*

I slam the sliding door of the van and run, dragging my four-year-old by the hand and unceremoniously lugging my one-year-old baby around to the front of Edman Chapel.

"Greta, sweetie, hurry up!" I urge.

She whines, "Mom, where are we going? Why so fast?"

"There is someone I want to see." How do you explain to a preschooler the need to see a rock star you have idolized since high school? "Sweetie, just trust me. Do this for Mommy. Hurry, hurry!"

We race around Edman Chapel, and we run into Juleen coming from the other direction.

"Where are your kids?" I ask incredulously, as we breathlessly run up the stairs and past the enormous white pillars.

"Jamie is at my house with them. Do you think Bono is here?"

We are both excited and full of anticipation as she opens the huge double doors. We burst into the atrium of the huge hall only to find it very calm. My heart sinks. We walk over to the doors leading to the auditorium. On the stage is Chaplain Kellough, talking in his characteristic monotone voice. "So we understand by this passage in the gospel of Matthew that we must ..."

I whisper slowly and with great disappointment, "That is definitely not Bono."

"No," Juleen moans. Shaking her head in mock disdain, she asks, "What are we doing?"

"Shhh." I giggle and scold, "I don't like that attitude."

We head back into the dreary November morning. A student is coming to chapel, apparently very late. "Hey!" I catch his attention. "Is Bono going to be here today?"

"Ah, yeah, he'll be here tonight."

"How are people getting in? Are there tickets?" I ask.

"They gave them to all the students. I don't think there are any left." He keeps walking and disappears into the building.

"Oh, well." Juleen sighs. "It was a fun adventure anyway."

"I'm getting in," I say resolutely and move Thomas from one hip to the other. He is squirming. "I'm sure someone has some tickets. Not all these kids care about Bono. They were *four* during the Joshua Tree tour. Honestly."

Juleen agrees and laughs. "Here's your chance. Chapel just let out."

We stand, two determined suburban mamas, facing a sea of college kids pouring out the four sets of double doors onto the courtyard. Unhindered by a baby on my hip and a confused four-year-old by my side, I start to accost the innocent. "Hey, do you have tickets to Bono? Are you going tonight?" I repeat this several times. No one is biting.

I eye an obvious freshman, a very young skinny collegiate unwittingly coming my way. "Hey!" I grab his arm. "Can I buy your Bono tickets off you?"

He is shocked and confused by a ticket-scalping mama. "Um," he stammers, "I have a ticket."

Determined to close the deal I push, "That's not good enough. I need two. What about your friend there?" I gesture toward a boy who stopped to observe the confrontation.

They glance at each other and are silent.

"OK, I'll give you forty bucks a ticket. Can you take a check?"

"Forty, really? I'll do that." They both light up. While I am writing the checks, they confess, "We didn't pay anything for the tickets. They came through campus mail."

Such cute, honest college boys.

"Well, then, enjoy!" I smile, hand them the checks, and give a little wave.

Feeling a bit guilty, but very pleased with myself, I gather my children and walk back to the car. I am pretty confident this is not what Bono had in mind when he planned the Heart of America tour. I think he would frown on two housewives scalping tickets off his target group. But the important thing is that I have my tickets.

I climb in the car with my mind full, wondering what the evening event will be like. I had just started to hear things about the AIDS crisis in Africa. It must be a bigger deal than I was aware of if it can prompt a rock icon to travel around the Midwest in a bus to raise awareness. I hurry home to arrange child care. I need to get in line at four. It is general seating and I am going to have a good seat.

●

I grew up hearing missionaries give presentations. I am a veteran of the slide show, the heartfelt testimonies, and the obligatory passing of the plate. Yet I am reeling from my ill-gotten evening with Bono. I was totally unprepared for what I heard that night.

I have no file in my brain for this information. No context. I am angry: Why have I never heard this? Why aren't we talking about this every Sunday in church? Where are the sermons and the offering plates for this pandemic? Why are we harping on the same things over and over from the pulpit, yet are ignorant of our neighbors' suffering?

Three hours of horrific things had been dumped in my lap—and I paid eighty bucks for it. I do not know what to do, and I am ashamed and angry at my ignorance. Processing the evening is not helped by the fact that today I am attending a suburban ritual—the Christmas cookie exchange.

"Oh, Shayne!" my current Christmas cookie exchange hostess chimes, "did you bring these white-chocolate-covered pretzels? They look delicious."

I murmur blandly, "Yup, those are mine." I quickly sort through cookies so I can head home. Thomas is in the basement with all the kids and is sorely in need of a nap.

"So, Juleen tells me you all went to see Bono at Wheaton. Was it okay?"

"What do you mean—was it *okay*?" I ask, distracted as I choose snickerdoodles and cut out sugar cookies to add to my plate.

"I heard he was . . . you know . . . he *swore*. In chapel!"

I lift my head and look at her very serious expression and let out a deep chuckle. "I know. It was awesome! I was so proud of Wheaton for having him come to speak."

Beth flips her hair and continues, "I don't know anything about this Bono, but I don't think Wheaton is the place to do that sort of thing. I mean, he's not a missionary or a pastor. I think it's dangerous to use a rock star—to set him up as someone to emulate. Especially for those young college students. I, personally, was very upset Wheaton allowed Bono and his show to come and perform."

Her attitude is par for the course in this subculture, as common as Christmas cookies. But tonight my guard is down and my heart is fragile and I'm spoiling for a fight.

"Were you there?" I ask.

"No, ah ... I've just heard things," Beth admits, backing off.

I say defensively, "It was a powerful night, with a powerful spirit. It profoundly affected me, and I'm quite sure it affected those college students as well."

"Oh, I'm sure it did," she said, trying to bring the conversation back to an appropriate cookie exchange level.

My heart is broken from the things I heard that night. I wince in sadness and frustration and continue, "You're not the first person I've heard this from. What's wrong with emulating Bono? I think it's so weird people have a hangup with a rock star calling people to action. Believe me, I would love to follow a pastor, but no one is leading when it comes to raising awareness about global AIDS."

As I add some gingerbread men to my plate far too aggressively, I look up and add, "Beth, there are people out there like Jim Wallis who have been trying to raise awareness. But where are our pastors? I have no problem if a rock star has to take their place." My frustrated tone wasn't scoring any points.

Besides, I can tell she doesn't know who Jim Wallis is.

My irritation is contagious. Beth smiles curtly and

says, "Well, I'm sure Bono will find some more like you out there."

I want to throw my snickerdoodles in her face.

•

I left the cookie exchange dejected. How am I any different from all those women in there? My daily schedule looks identical to theirs. I am a stay-at-home mom whose full-time job is to take care of my family. I cook homemade meals. I do mountains of laundry every week. I go to cookie exchanges and make nice-nice and pretend to care about potty training, what sports team the kids did or did not make, and manicures.

I admit it. I didn't care too much about what Bono was going to talk about when I scalped tickets to see him. His star power drew me. I dump my Christmas cookies on the front seat of my minivan, then return to fetch my one-year-old. As I buckle Thomas into his car seat, my thoughts turn to Agnes, a woman from Nigeria. Agnes Nyamayarwo was part of Bono's Heart of America tour. She seemed out of place on the stage in the huge hall, seated next to Chris Rock and Ashley Judd. I think she may have even fallen asleep at one point in the presentation.

Agnes was dressed humbly in clothes that didn't fit her very well and huge black shoes. Her body language was static. She told her story in a thick, weary accent — eventually my ears grew accustomed, and I heard a story of tremendous loss. Agnes lost her entire family to AIDS — her entire extended family, her husband, and her children. Her youngest son died at age six.

My oldest son is six.

When Bono finally came on the stage, the crowd was sobered and attentive. I've grown up deeply entrenched in the Protestant world. I was a fifth-generation undergraduate student at Wheaton, my father was a professor, and my grandfather was with Youth for Christ at its inception and worked with Billy Graham as his music director. I know the best and the worst my tradition has to offer — and that night was one of the best.

In the heart of the conservative Christian academy, a rock icon shared about how his heart was broken when he learned about the global AIDS crisis. He shared his conviction that if 8,000 people were dying a day in Paris or New York from AIDS, we would be hearing about it on the news every night. He challenged us to ask why we aren't aware of what is going on in Africa. Bono's talk was short. Simple. He dropped the f-bomb once and said *hell* a couple times in a context entirely new to the stage of Edman Chapel. Running through my mind the whole time was the refrain: *Why hasn't anyone in church told me this before? Why have I never heard this?*

At one point, Bono pulled out a guitar and a boom box and began to sing a song called "American Prayer":

> *Remember that what you see depends on where you stand*
> *... let's not get tired*
> *Let's not kick at the darkness*
> *Let's make the light brighter*
> *These are the hands*
> *What are we going to build with them?*

Bono's all-too-familiar voice filled the chapel. This song—these lyrics—after everything I had just heard, was almost too much. I felt oversaturated with information, emotions, and my own thoughts.

Just when I thought my emotional tank could not take one more thing, Bono did something that fully woke up the sleeping woman and the compassion from deep within me. He called the American church to action. A non-American, non-evangelical, non-mainstream Christian stood on the stage of an elite Christian liberal arts college and took the role of prophet, calling the church to action.

"If the church doesn't respond to the plagues of Africa, who will?"

There was no predictable five-step program we could sign up for to help fix it. There was no typical request for donations. No prayer sheet we could take home to soothe our consciences. The facts were simply dumped in our laps.

Home from the cookie exchange, I pull into my driveway and park. As I get out of the front seat of my minivan, I notice the seat next to me is covered in cookie crumbs. I unbuckle Thomas and manage to carry him in his awkward snowsuit and my new plate of Christmas cookies into the house. Feeling decidedly nonfestive, I settle Thomas in the ExerSaucer and plop my cookies on the counter. I move to the sink to attempt to do something about the pile of dishes, but I stand and stare out the window instead.

Letting out a crushing sigh, I think, *Who am I kidding? I'm not a pastor or a rock star. I'm just a housewife. Who am I to make a difference? My voice is so small.*

- In 2002, only 5 percent of evangelical Christians were willing to donate money for global AIDS relief or education.[1]
- In 2007, HIV/AIDS killed 2.1 million people and 2.5 million people were newly infected with the virus.[2]
- There are 22.5 million people living with HIV in Africa alone.[3]
- Every day in Africa, 4,400 people die as a result of HIV/AIDS and 4,700 people become newly infected with the virus.[4]
- In South Africa alone, nearly one in every five children are projected to be orphaned by 2010.[5]
- Africa has been hit harder by HIV/AIDS than any other region in the world; over two-thirds of people living with and dying from HIV are in Africa.[6]

4

WHAT IS A NICE SOCCER MOM DOING IN A PLACE LIKE THIS?

Scripture sheds light on the why of poverty by addressing issues of greed, disobedience, isolation, and discrimination, but ultimately the power to overcome poverty and disease lies not so much in assigning blame as in learning to live the Jesus way; to follow him in how he interacted with the poor and suffering, to take up our cross of loving generosity, kindness, and tenacious advocacy for the poor and oppressed.

Arloa Sutter, president,
Breakthrough Urban Ministries

ILLINOIS, 2002

I slowly sip my cup of room-temperature coffee. It is watery and bitter, but at least it's a socially acceptable prop I can hide behind.

Today I was able to catch the first half of my son's soccer game before meeting up with Juleen. "I'm glad this worked out. I'm glad you came with me," I whisper in her ear. Juleen gives a knowing smile. We are thinking the same thing, *What the heck are we doing here?*

Here is a room full of Franciscan Sisters, and not another soccer mom in sight. There are a few men scattered throughout the room. The tables are full of people, and the room is buzzing as everyone visits with one another and helps themselves to coffee and pastries.

I feel out of place, but I'm trying to be attentive and watchful. Just last week I sat through the heart-wrenching four-hour presentation of Bono's Heart of America tour. As the last speaker sat down that night, Wheaton College's Chaplain Kellough took the podium. "We would like to thank the Franciscan Sisters for partnering to make this evening possible," he said.

Franciscan Sisters? It had only been a month since my encounter with the convent and the cosmic statue of Saint Francis. The nerve endings of my soul fired again, finding this an unlikely coincidence. Since when do local Catholics and Protestants partner to bring a rock star to their town to talk about poverty and AIDS? A month ago, I had no idea of the work of the Franciscan Sisters, even though they lived and ministered down the road from my house.

Chaplain Kellough had continued with: "We hope to keep the spirit of this evening alive and keep the momentum going. There will be an advocacy group starting up on campus. There will also be a community group beginning on the campus of the Franciscan Sisters. Please contact Sister Sheila Kinsey for more information."

So here I was.

"I am so pleased to welcome you all today to the first DGAAN meeting," says a spunky nun with short white hair. "My name is Sister Sheila Kinsey, and I am the director for the Franciscan Sisters' Justice, Peace, and Integrity of Creation Office."

Of course she is, I think, remembering my tour of the convent with Sister Gabrielle.

This smiling woman is dressed in a blue blazer and a T-shirt with "JUBILEE: Drop the Debt" emblazoned across it. She has my full attention. Her connection to this mysterious office, her intelligent smile, and the deep light in her eyes pull me deeper into this conversation God seems to be having with me.

Sister Sheila says, "DGAAN stands for the DuPage Glocal AIDS Action Network. The word *Glocal* is an amalgam of *global* and *local*. This is to symbolize our awareness that poverty and the HIV/AIDS pandemic must be addressed on both the local and global levels.

"As you know, we are gathered here to continue the

spirit and good work of Bono's Heart of America tour. Prior to that meeting, many of us — seventy-five community leaders — were invited by VIP ticket to meet and discuss the HIV/AIDS pandemic in Africa."

I look around the room at all the unfamiliar faces. I am suddenly acutely aware of my non-VIP-community-leader status. Involuntarily, I raise my coffee cup in front of my face with the hopes no one will notice me.

"In 2000, world leaders at the United Nations committed to eight goals to alleviate global poverty called the Millennium Development Goals." Sister Sheila gives a small wave. "Hi, Dave, nice to see you. Dave has done extensive work with Jubilee USA. Really, it's an honor to have you here today. We all know the work Jubilee has done in working toward dropping the debt of impoverished nations, another key component in eradicating AIDS and extreme poverty in the developing world. The G8 leaders, under pressure from the global Jubilee movement, canceled the debt for several countries in 1999."

As people applaud, I glance at Juleen with eyebrows raised as if to say, "I have no idea what this woman is talking about." My embarrassment flares again, along with anger — *why don't I know these things?* I am irritated my church and my friends are not part of this dialogue, irritated at myself that I haven't been part of it. As I look around the room, I wonder if Juleen and I are the only nondenominational Protestants here — two random suburban housewives.

Sister Sheila continues, "We will continue to have DGAAN meetings every two months, to work together in our various arenas supporting the Millennium Development Goals. Our goal is to build a strong advocate voice in the DuPage County area and to expand that voice into local, national, and international arenas.

"We strive to find ways to network successfully and build an enduring community. We are unusual as a community because we cross boundaries; we are different people from different backgrounds — Catholic, Episcopal, Lutheran, Quaker, Democrat and Republican, black and white, gay and straight, students and community leaders. We hope to be a broad network crossing social, religious, and political barriers to form bonds and realize our differences can complement rather than conflict."

I cannot help but notice that "stay-at-home mom" does not make her list.

Sister Sheila gestures to a nun next to her. "I would now like to introduce Sister Florence Muia. Sister Florence is starting a ministry to women and children living with HIV and AIDS in her home country of Kenya."

Sister Florence steps to the microphone. "It took about fifteen years of silence on HIV and an AIDS epidemic in my country before the then president of Kenya, Mr. Daniel arap Moi, acknowledged HIV and AIDS as a 'national disaster' in 1999. The many years of silence saw the disease take root in the country. Watching all the suffering, I did not want to sit on the other side of the fence. I realized that I needed to establish a Kenyan project by and for the Kenyan people. My vision was for a safe haven for women, men, and children affected by the disease. I call this sanctuary 'Upendo Village.' *Upendo* means 'love' in Kiswahili language."

Juleen looks over at me and smiles.

Sister Florence continues, "Upendo Village has provided home-based care to many people in the community of Naivasha, Kenya. The staff strives to give love, care, and support to those who have been devastated by AIDS, using resources from donors and friends of the village who share our dream." Sister Florence looks at the clock. "Well, I am sure I have used up all my time. Thank you."

Sister Sheila adjusts the microphone. "I would now like to invite you to network with one another. I know some of you are tracking the IMF and the WHO. Is Timothy here to talk about the Global Fund? Sandra, do you have some words on DOHA? Oh, good. Thank you all again for coming."

DGAAN, MDG, IMF, WHO, Jubilee, Global Fund, DOHA, Upendo Village? These acronyms are making my eyes glaze over. Network with one another? Can someone define the terms first? Juleen and I look at each other, smile, and shrug. We don't speak or move from our seats. We have no idea what to do.

As people begin to mill around, I remain attentive, hoping to get some kind of guidance. This room full of strange faces and heady conversations is way outside my arena. This is my hometown. In some circles I feel as if I know *everybody*. I joke I could walk into any church in town and know a handful of people, but here in this assembly I feel like a fish out of water. This is a new world, and I am still standing on the shore.

"I work with World Vision. My name is Tony Frank." I overhear an introduction.

I breathe a sigh of relief. Having grown up in the church, I am familiar with World Vision, a Christian humanitarian organization that works with children, families, and communities worldwide. They are dedicated to helping all people reach their full potential by tackling the causes of poverty and injustice. Through World Vision, my husband and I sponsor two children in Zambia.

If World Vision is involved in this movement, maybe I could be too.

●

That first meeting was incredibly uncomfortable. I kept waiting for someone to walk up to me, ask me a question, and, upon realizing my ineptness, blurt out, "What are *you* doing here?"

However, taking the risk to show up yielded fruit. I kept going, kept praying, and kept learning. I couldn't deny God's clear call to me to be involved in helping the poorest of the poor around the world, and if God wanted this soccer mom to show up every Saturday morning at the local Franciscan convent, then so be it.

Slowly I began to find my place. The community advocacy group DGAAN was my doorway into the complicated and multilayered world of global advocacy and policy. I still feel overwhelmed at my ignorance—global HIV/AIDS and extreme poverty are monstrous issues—but now I'm part of the conversation.

Despite feeling overwhelmed and shamed at my ignorance, I decided it would be worse to curl up and forget about it than to just dive in—ignorance and all. I could not imagine having to tell my children in thirty years, after my generation has handed this mess to them, "Oh, yeah, I guess I did hear something about that back then, but I never did anything about it."

Through DGAAN I became one of the original members of the ONE Campaign: The Campaign to Make Poverty History. When Bono brought the Heart of America tour to my town, ONE did not exist. DATA had been formed by people like Bono and Bobby Shriver, and it stands for Debt, AID, Trade, and Africa. DATA is a very sophisticated research group, and they keep tabs on what governments are doing or not doing in the fight against global poverty. DATA helps create global policies around issues of debt, aid, and trade, putting pressure on developed nations, like the United States and Britain, to do their part in the fight against extreme poverty in Africa.

The movement continued to grow and in 2004, DATA, along with other large antipoverty organizations such as Bread for the World, CARE USA, Oxfam, and World Vision, joined together to create a new nonpartisan campaign to mobilize Americans from all walks of life to fight extreme poverty and preventable global disease. Hence, the ONE Campaign was launched with the support of celebrities, pastors, and ordinary Americans.

The meetings with DGAAN are vibrant and productive. We work in the community, raising awareness, telephoning our representatives in Congress, and supporting each other's causes. We gained the attention of those in Washington, D.C. In fact, in that first year, leaders of DATA and ONE came back to our DGAAN meetings to thank us for our support and to tell us about the newly formed ONE Campaign.

By networking with my community, I also got involved with World Vision in a deeper way. World Vision is a huge nongovernment organization working in hundreds of developing nations across the world. In fact, it has the largest infrastructure of any humanitarian organization. World Vision is a tangible bridge to the poorest of the poor, and this caught my imagination for the possibilities of how I could get involved. Through World Vision, I sponsor a child in an area of the world ravaged by extreme poverty and AIDS.

As I continued to educate myself, I was given opportunities to share with others. Every October, organizations that share concern for these causes stage "Stand Up for Poverty" rallies around the United States. One year I was invited to speak at the Chicago rally. I was humbled and excited because my involvement, even though I don't work for any of these organizations, was still valuable. They wanted a mom's voice at the rally.

That evening, my whole family went with me to the city. My five-year-old, Thomas, ran around the oak-paneled room at the Chicago Cultural Center with dozens of ONE bands (those white plastic bracelets that have ONE imprinted on them) on each arm. My husband and my three kids sat in the audience and listened as I shared with hundreds of people why ONE, World Vision, and DGAAN are so important to me and some of the significant and life-changing things I have learned. I still remember standing at the podium with my kids' faces looking at me and smiling as I urged the room to stand up in solidarity with the poorest of the poor.

- Advocacy is the pursuit of influencing outcomes — including public policy and resource allocation decisions within political, economic, and social systems and institutions — that directly affect people's current lives.[1]
- In 1980, Africa had a 6 percent share of world trade. By 2005, this had dropped to less than 2 percent.[2]
- Debt relief and aid targeted to education helped send 29 million more African children to school between 1999 and 2005.[3]

5

WE DON'T KNOW WHAT WE'RE DOING, BUT WE KNOW WE'RE DOING SOMETHING

Somehow she seemed more than my daughter; she was my mother, my grandmother, and myself. She was every woman ever born, bent and contained in a small, ageless cameo that bore the truth about "a woman's place."

Sue Monk Kidd, Dance of the Dissident Daughter

Glen Ellyn, Illinois, 2003

"Do you think anyone will show up?" I ask Juleen as I arrange scones and croissants on the serving table.

Juleen pulls her enormous mane of blond hair away from her face and looks at me with her contagious sparkle. "I have no idea," she says, shaking her head and laughing at me.

"How do I always end up doing these crazy things with you?" I tease, throwing an M&M at her.

The truth is, Juleen and I share a heart for those who are suffering. In fact, Juleen Ritchie is my hero in the faith. If it weren't too cliché, I'd call her my soul mate. Her soul knows my soul, and the safety of this friendship has been life to me over the years. Ever since we became friends in college, Juleen has had an intimate and unwavering relationship with God.

Juleen has known real struggle and suffering as a mother. I have watched her raise a special-needs child — her patience, endurance, and her relentless belief that God is with her in it all has humbled me. I feel blessed to have journeyed these years with her, and I am continually struck by the depth of her faith and dependence on God. Juleen's influence and story have been treasured companions to me.

"Seriously," I ask, "what if *no one* shows up?"

Juleen can't respond since my question has sent her into

a laughing fit, which soon spreads to me. Doubled over and in tears, we finally pull it together.

"Ah, well ..."—Juleen takes a deep breath, wiping tears from her startling blue eyes—"we'll be eating Suzette's pastries for like a month." She picks up a scone to take a bite.

Juleen and I are hosting a tea to honor Princess Kasune Zulu of Zambia. Working with World Vision, we invited Princess to come and tell her story to our friends. We chose a local community center—the Boathouse in Glen Ellyn—with a large open room and a wall of windows looking out over a small lake. The old knotty cedar siding and fireplace make it a cozy, charming space.

Lake Ellyn is surrounded by sprawling lawns, hundred-year-old trees, and a picturesque old school. As a girl in junior high and high school, I rode my bike to this peaceful place to connect with nature and with God. This was usually when I was in some kind of coming-of-age angst. I sat by the water to pray and to cast my worries—symbolized by whatever was at hand, from Hershey's Kisses to a bologna sandwich—into the water in a self-made ceremony of necessity.

Now as a woman, Lake Ellyn is still my cathedral. God continues to show up for me here—but now I'm wondering if anyone else will show up for this tea.

I stare apprehensively over the expansive lawn, dotted with huge maple and oak trees, when I notice women starting to trickle down toward the Boathouse. My heart starts to pump a little faster. People are really coming.

Through the community meetings at the Franciscan convent, Juleen and I connected with Tony Frank of World Vision. Tony introduced us to Princess Kasune Zulu, a new member of the World Vision Chicago team, a wife and mother from Zambia, and a woman who is HIV positive. Princess is one of the most beautiful people I have ever met—she simply *owns* her own skin. She speaks and moves with grace and confidence, and she has an intelligent and playful sense of humor that transcends any cultural barriers.

Princess is her given first name, but you'd be forgiven for thinking she is royalty. In fact, Princess has royal lineage through her father and the Lenje tribe. She wears the traditional Zambian attire: a full fabric skirt, blouse, and scarf all in a bright royal blue and gold matching pattern. She has a beautiful, joyful face, and her ebony skin is perfection. Princess has the intangible gift of standing out and blending in all at the same time. I was immediately comfortable with Princess, and our conversation flowed effortlessly.

Princess makes it very clear that she has been released from the shame and stigma of being HIV positive, and she considers it her calling to educate and share a message of hope to others living with HIV and AIDS. Her confidence in this is something one cannot fake, and I am quickly caught up by her accent, the lilt of her laugh, the engaging fire in her eyes, and the power of her story.

"When I found out I had the virus, I was filled with joy. I don't know why—it was a death sentence," says Princess. "Growing up in Zambia, I lost my brother and my baby sister to AIDS. Then AIDS claimed my mother, then my father. At seventeen, I dropped out of school. I got pregnant. At eighteen, I married my boyfriend, a man twenty-five years older than me. He had already lost two wives suspected of having AIDS. I am now HIV positive."

As Princess shares her story, I am reminded that these are the facts of life in sub-Saharan Africa, where 6,000 people die every day from AIDS.

"I only realized that my parents died of AIDS much later on in my life," she says, "when I started reading books and magazines and watching shows on TV about AIDS."

The dishes had long since been cleared and my coffee is room temperature when Princess confesses, "When I found out I was HIV positive and how it is spread, I started going along the highways, pretending to be a prostitute, in hopes a truck driver would pick me up and I could tell him about the disease."

"What?" I am stunned. "You would be picked up because they thought you were a prostitute ... and then what?"

"I would tell them it is not safe to drive the roads and have many sexual partners before returning home to their wives. I would educate them and tell them my status and tell them they need to stop this behavior."

"Princess!" I am stunned and impressed, but I say, "That is *not* safe!"

Chuckling, she responds, "Well, no one else is talking about it, and it must be talked about. Women need to be protected somehow. In Zambia it is hard for a woman to make her husband wear a condom if he refuses."

The juxtaposition of being so comfortable with someone, as if you have been lifelong friends, with the incredibly foreign story I am hearing is an emotional, wild ride. Yet what Princess shared next was so confrontational to my suburban life as a wife and mother, I have never been the same.

Princess said, "When I first suspected I contracted the virus from my husband, I wanted to go get tested, but in Zambia a wife cannot get tested without the permission, without a signature from the husband. And so for a long while I could not find out my status or the status of my children because my husband would not sign."

Her reality shook me. And I thought, *How is this possible that women around the world are still treated this way? This could be me. This could be my life. But it's not—and only because of where I happened to be born.*

I met Princess in 2002, when the global HIV/AIDS pandemic was just beginning to come to the forefront of awareness with governments and churches. It was not prominently discussed on the news, not at the national level or the multinational government level and certainly not in churches. Meeting Princess and getting to know her story did something to me. It knocked the suburban breath right out of me.

I've always been aware that I live in a bubble—junior high, high school, and college all in the same Midwestern town. So right after college, I moved to South Central Los Angeles to teach at an inner-city school. This time expanded my understanding of things non-middle-America and gave me time to develop my compassion muscle. In the inner city, I had to come to terms with the messiness of poverty and all the complex issues and causes. I built relationships with people very different from me, and I grew in deep compassion as I journeyed with them and experienced the hard realities of life in the inner city.

It had been years since my time in South Central L.A. After being married, I wanted to live in my hometown and raise my family here. I got a job teaching junior high in a neighboring town, and then I stayed home after the birth of my first son. I settled back into comfortable suburbia without much conflict. I was a young wife and a young mother and I was building a life of security and safety for myself and my family. To be honest, there was no connection to my life in the inner city of Los Angeles in my life as a new stay-at-home mom. L.A. was on the other side of the country, and my babies, along with my other stay-at-home mom friends, my church, and Bible studies — these were the things in front of me.

My days filled up with the concerns of making sure my three babies were fed, clean, and well behaved. My stresses were around things like strep throat that won't go away, or finding those darn inserts for the sippy cups, or digging through the dirty clothes to find the least dirty onesie until I could get some laundry done. I spent non-naptime hours at the parks and tot lots with other stay-at-home moms and their kids.

I have a group of friends, some I have known since junior high, and we would meet every Wednesday to pray for one another. This time became a lifeline to me — sanity in the midst of the busyness and chaos of managing a family with small children. We shared our lives, our struggles, and our secrets for making this time a bit easier or more efficient. We were so desperate to connect and feel the support of other women that we still laugh about the day we met at Juleen's house when, combined, we had almost fifteen children under the age of three. We had no babysitter that day, and children ran around the house, wiggled under our feet, crawled over us and the furniture while babies sprawled across laps—and we were all unfazed by it. We continued to talk and pray together in the din of total insanity.

It was these women, and others with whom we shared this time of life, that Juleen and I had invited to hear Princess. Waking up to the realities of the AIDS situation in sub-Saharan Africa and building a relationship with Princess was unnervingly connecting my present life with my past life in the inner city. For years my compassion muscle had been busy caring for my own babies, but now God was growing something in me. My compassion was waking up and expanding, and I knew I could never go back to being neutral about things that break my heart. And even though I didn't know what we were doing, I knew we had to do *something*—I didn't know where it was all going, but I had a deep sense that I was simply to keep moving forward. I knew, or I longed to believe, that if other women heard this story and met this beautiful sister, they too would never be the same.

The women—church members, book club members, old coworkers, friends, and parents of friends—are filing through the refreshment line, piling their plates with croissants, cookies, and chocolates. Juleen leans against the wall, chatting easily with an old friend, occasionally looking at me to giggle as I fuss with portions, run back and forth to the kitchen, and vivaciously greet every single person.

Soon we sit down and begin. Princess addresses the room — packed with eighty women! — saying, "HIV knows no boundaries."

As I listened to Princess's story for the third time, I was reminded of what made me fall in love with her: strength. Her strength does not come from a culture that went through social movements like women's suffrage or the civil-rights movement; her strength flows simply from the depths of who God made her to be.

Princess gently taught us while she shared her journey with HIV and AIDS. She told us that the rate of HIV infection is higher among girls and women than it is among men. In Africa, virtually every infected woman contracts HIV from a male partner with whom she cannot choose to abstain from sex. Studies show that women, and particularly young girls, are more vulnerable to contracting the HIV virus. The genital lining can easily be broken and increases chances of infection. Not only are women biologically more vulnerable, they are socially more vulnerable. Women are more likely to be coerced into sex or raped, and they have no say in condom use. Many young girls have sexual relations with much older men, who lure them with gifts and favors.

Women lack a voice, and the price of that silence is the continuing spread of HIV and AIDS. UNAIDS reports three-fourths of all the women living with HIV and AIDS live in the developing world. In many of these societies, women have few rights in the sexual relationship and within the family structure. Men come home and refuse to wear condoms. This makes it difficult for a woman to protect herself against HIV and to protect her children. Men make all major decisions within a household, including the decision to have more than one sexual partner.

Patriarchal social structures can harm women of all ages. In a family where there are sick people, caring for the ill is the women's job, often in addition to other work that can bring in money. When the mother and the father are sick, young girls become the main caregivers, which causes them to drop out of school. This disproportionate expectation placed on women and young girls increases risky sexual behavior, which is often seen as a way to make a living or simply survive. In Africa, the rate of infection in teenage girls is six times higher than in women over thirty-five. About one in four teenage girls lives with HIV, compared with one in twenty-five teenage boys.

Princess is blessed that even though she is woman, she was able to be educated in Zambia. She explains education is the most effective way to prevent HIV infection in women and girls. If every child in the developing world received a basic primary education, about 700,000 new HIV infections would be prevented yearly, especially in girls. Schools can teach HIV prevention methods such as condom use, encouraging fewer (or no) sexual partners, and the importance of discussing HIV and AIDS openly. UNAIDS has stated that girls who attend school are more likely able to make sexual decisions for themselves, are more independent, and are more likely to earn an income. Increased education will also help reduce the cultural stigma of HIV and AIDS.

Being taught these things by Princess stirred the hearts of many women. Our tea was only a drop in the bucket, but it was still a drop—a step we took to follow God's call in our lives instead of doing nothing. Several months later, Princess found herself in the White House meeting President George W. Bush and Secretary of State Colin Powell. She, along with national leaders, urged President Bush to pass the AIDS bill and PEPFAR. Since I first met Princess, she has met with senior leaders from the British and Irish parliaments, her own president of Zambia, Mrs. Mandela from South Africa, and ambassadors from many countries. She has been featured in *USA Today*, the *Wall Street Journal*, and *Christianity Today*, and she wrote a book about how she emerged an unexpected champion for those at risk and affected by AIDS called *Warrior Princess*.

During the year following the tea, the women we'd assembled gave money through World Vision so Princess could return to Zambia and produce her own nationally syndicated radio series. Women may not talk about issues of sex, fidelity, justice, and HIV/AIDS with one another, but everyone is thinking about it. Radio is the most effective way of getting the message out to women who feel trapped and scared. A woman can clean her home and cook her meals while hearing a message of hope. Princess's program, called *Positive Living*, was broadcast in English and seven other languages, and it received honors from the U.S. embassy in Zambia for excellence in broadcasting on HIV and AIDS.

I didn't expect a fellow mother to provide a model of grassroots global social advocacy—especially a mother from the other side of the world. Princess became a compelling guide on how to fight overwhelming odds with a brave, hopeful heart. Princess is not an angry, militant, placard-waving activist; she is a smart, intentional, feisty activist who stands on an unmovable foundation of love, hope, and justice. Such a foundation cannot be shaken and is stronger than any oppressive forces that may try to come against it, even death.

As Princess finishes her presentation, I glance out the window of the Boathouse and across the glinting surface of the lake. Couples are walking their dogs and men are fishing. A woman pushes a stroller along the paved path. The ladies laugh as Princess tells an anecdote about cultures clashing. I turn from the window to look at her, and I am amazed. How did this happen? How is there a room full of Midwesterners, who would normally never assemble, anxious to hear a Zambian woman share her story?

The sun pours through the paned windows, dramatically lighting the room, and I realize I know the answer to my own question. Each woman came because she was invited. In this moment, something clicks in me. I begin to understand the power of grassroots organizing. I acted in my sphere of influence to tell a story and to hope for change.

- Women have lost control of their bodies and their lives. In many societies, women gain freedom from the wishes of their fathers only when power over them is handed to their husbands.[1]
- Statistics reveal that girls and young women remain far more vulnerable to HIV infection than young men, with two-thirds of the 5.5 million fifteen- through twenty-four-year-olds with HIV worldwide being women. The majority of these young people still lack comprehensive and correct information about how to prevent HIV infection or do not have the power to act on that knowledge.[2]
- At least 12.1 million African children have lost one or both parents to AIDS.[3]

A DIALOGUE
LED BY LOVE

Every stereotype can be broken with a face, and every face has a story. Even leaders in both the gay community and the Christian community tell me they know that something needs to change—but nothing is changing because we've all been conditioned to dig in and fight.

Andrew Marin, Love Is an Orientation

Now this was the sin of your sister Sodom: She and her daughters were arrogant, overfed and unconcerned; they did not help the poor and needy.

Ezekiel 16:49

CHICAGO, 2008

The sun is unusually hot and bright this October morning. It bounces off the skyscrapers, and the skyline facing the lake glows. There is little wind coming in off Lake Michigan — not enough to cool off the thousands of participants at this year's 5K Chicago AIDS walk/run. I need to find Brad and the Mosaic Initiative team, but I'm stuck in line waiting to get my T-shirt and number.

While pinning on my number, I catalog the many walks of life around me. Ahead of me is a respected South Side pastor and his congregation. At the top of the hill, a pack of Loyola students in matching yellow T-shirts, complete with cheerleader and megaphone, cavort and shout. Gay and lesbian couples walk past, as well as straight families with strollers.

I am surprised by the normalcy of the whole thing. This is my first Chicago AIDS walk/run, and whatever I was expecting, it wasn't this. Maybe I thought there would be more hot pink boas and tank tops? As I push my way through the crowd, still looking for my team, I am uncomfortably confronted with my own preconceptions. Around me are Chicagoans who took the time to show up because they want to fight the suffering caused by HIV and AIDS ... not just people from the gay and lesbian community. I see mothers and fathers, grandmothers and grandfathers. I pass a cluster of high school students, and I almost trip over a toddler running across the path.

AIDS gained recognition in the United States back in the 1980s when alarming numbers of gay men began to die from the mysterious virus. Many people lost their friends, brothers, and sons. It was a sorrowful time in our history that is not talked about much anymore. Today, AIDS is still a threat — despite advances in prevention and treatment — and not only to the gay community. For instance, in Illinois today there are over 40,000 people living with HIV and perhaps over 10,000 people undiagnosed. And 76 percent of women living with HIV contracted it from sex with a man. Over 66 percent of the people living with HIV and AIDS in Illinois live in Chicago.

I met Brad while attending my first DGAAN community meetings, where I was learning to be an advocate for the global AIDS crisis. In a time when there is heated debate between the church and the gay community, Brad and his organization, along with the churches involved with DGAAN, crossed this treacherous bridge and created real relationships with one another. In an age where disdain, disrespect, and hate dominate the conversation between the two sides, our little band of DGAAN members who meet on Saturday mornings somehow escaped this trap. Brad had become a good friend and someone I look up to in this journey.

As a Quaker, Brad always brought a unique perspective to our time together. He was the director of Canticle Ministries, a Franciscan organization helping people with HIV/AIDS in DuPage County, Illinois, find housing, community support, and education. While many of the participants at our meetings were focused on the AIDS pandemic in sub-Saharan Africa, Brad consistently brought the conversation to a both/and level — passionately and persistently reminding us the AIDS crisis is not only happening on the other side of the world. The AIDS crisis is also a serious domestic issue that gets very little attention or press here in America — even as it devastates entire families and communities. With intelligence and a wry sense of humor, Brad is the kind of person who can talk to — and listen to — almost anyone.

Brad had recently moved to Washington, D.C., to work with William Penn House, so I was looking forward to seeing him and catching up. We settle into a nice stride along Lake Michigan's waterfront. The event route would take us along Grant Park, past the Shedd Aquarium, and wind us toward Navy Pier before ending back at the park.

Brad is working on making home HIV tests as accessible and commonplace as drugstore pregnancy tests. For a number of reasons, these tests are a big deal and not yet approved by our government. Expressing his frustration, Brad says, "I was diagnosed with HIV in 1993. I got tested fully expecting to be negative. I was healthy, active, and knew that the only time I could have been exposed to HIV was in the mid-1980s. When the doctor came in the room to give me the results, she asked me how I got HIV. I just looked at her, trying not to cry."

Brad pauses. I glance at him to see if he might be crying now. Catching me, he admits, "It was a horrible and humiliating experience. The doctor asked, 'Are you homosexual?' I said, 'Yes,' and she said, 'Well, that's why.'" Brad mimics the curtness of her voice.

I cringe as Brad continues, "She gave no information about what to expect, said there were really no effective treatments available, and I just needed to wait until I got sick."

I understand any words I might offer cannot undo the pain of that moment, so I remain quiet.

"You know, when I found out my status," Brad confides, "I left the clinic and went outside. The sun was setting and it was a beautiful sunset. I stood on the sidewalk, and an overwhelming presence of God came over me. I can't explain it except that in that moment I knew everything was going to be all right. God was with me. I had a profound sense of peace."

●

Brad was my first gay friend. It's not that I was hiding from or ignoring gay people, but for the last decade or so I have been living in the mecca of evangelicalism. My social circles just didn't bring me in contact with the gay community. Evangelicals and gays usually make a point of staying away from each other.

In fact, the relationship between the church and the gay community is too often a hostile one. Conservative Christians maintain that a gay lifestyle is a choice and that the Bible teaches it is a sin. The gay community maintains that sexual orientation is not a choice, gay men and women were born gay, that it is not a sin, and claims the Bible is neutral on the expression of the gay lifestyle as we see it in today's world. These two groups seem only to be growing further apart. The gay community perceives conservative Christians as bigoted, closed-minded hypocrites who say they have the love of Christ but who treat and interact with the gay community in ways anything but loving. And the Christian community perceives gays as a threat to our society, our family values, and the church.

The scary thing is, the fight against AIDS and the struggle to prevent HIV transmission has only just begun, and I can't help but wonder, *Why can Brad and I get along, as different as we are?* I mean, Brad has strong opinions and he is not timid about voicing them. I don't agree with everything he says. Sometimes I don't agree with *anything* he says, but he's okay with that and so am I. It is the dialogue that is important. The relationship being built and the gesture of an attempt to understand one another — this is what really matters to both of us.

When the fire was first lit in me to understand the AIDS crisis and to be an advocate, I was very naïve. I believed if caring Christians heard and really understood the magnitude of what was going on, both at the global level and also right here in our own backyards, people's response would be as gung ho as my own. But time and time again, while trying to mobilize local congregations, I found this was not the case.

One of the churches I spoke to is run by committee, and I was invited to attend the community outreach meeting and present what was going on locally with Brad, Canticle Ministries, and the Mosaic Initiative, and how this congregation might get involved. I educated them about the local HIV/AIDS community and opportunities to help, such as providing meals and other support. World AIDS Day, which is held December 1 annually, was coming up, and I invited this church to participate in the local ecumenical worship service.

My presentation was met with glassy eyes, no sign of compassion, and no desire to be involved. In fact, I would say the topic of getting involved with the local HIV population was such an uncomfortable thought to most people around the table that anyone could have seen what I saw— the minute I passed out my handout, the collective body language radically changed to a stance of defensiveness. I never had a chance.

Sometime later, the pastor of community outreach followed up with me. He is a sincere man with a huge heart. He thanked me, but admitted his congregation was just not ready to take this step yet. I remember wondering, *Ready for what? We spent most of that meeting carrying on about why prayer should be brought back into schools, but we are not ready to care about our neighbors who are dying? We are not ready to care about people because we disagree with them and we believe deep down they got AIDS from sinful behavior and so that justifies not getting involved?*

My frustration with my faith tradition continued to mount when an event was planned to raise awareness about global HIV and AIDS. A large conservative Christian organization planned a dinner and concert which included speakers. While many of us who attended the DGAAN meetings and who worked in town were asked to present, Brad was excluded. It was an obvious snub. He wasn't invited because he is gay.

Brad admitted to me it was hurtful and discouraging to be passed over. I care for Brad, and I mourned the fact that my community had hurt him. I asked for forgiveness on behalf of my faith tradition. I expressed regret that not everyone understands how to do what he can do so effortlessly — build bridges of relationship with people with whom he passionately disagrees. I explained to him that before I met him, I had never seen it done.

Brad is gifted this way. Yes, he is a gay man living with HIV, which securely places him in the liberal camp of ideology and theology. But he is not partisan, if you will. Brad has webs of respectful relationships running deep into all kinds of "camps" — Democrats, Republicans, progressives, conservatives. He speaks with candor and strong opinion into his *own* communities where he sees injustice, disrespectful attitudes, poorly based arguments, and irresponsible behavior. And he has earned the permission to do this because he chooses relationship over being right.

In the majority of conservative churches and communities, the homosexual issue is a real fight and it scares people, as it is a threat to values of biblical living. In the majority of liberal churches and in the gay community, it's a real fight, and I think it's scary to them too — that people would treat them poorly based on sexual behavior. I have come to believe most people on the polarizing sides of the debate do not know any *people* who are actually a part of the story. It is ideology, theology, opinion, and prejudice that run the show. Both sides are guilty of digging in their heels, of committing verbal abuse, of writing the other side off, and regarding one another with great hostility.

●

Brad turns around to laugh at a comment from one of our fellow AIDS walk team members. I take a deep breath, enjoying the day, the conversation, the sun on Lake Michigan, and the sound of rigging clanking against sailboat masts in the harbor.

Brad and I had been discussing some of his frustrations with the gay and Quaker communities and their stance at times with fighting HIV and AIDS. We were commiserating over the sluggish response, the defensiveness, and the openly hostile rhetoric in both our communities.

Brad turns back to me. "Here's the thing, Shayne. We all draw lines in the sand on issues, but I have come to believe that our most important allies are not those on *our* side of the line, but those just on the *other* side." He speeds up our pace to pass some slower walkers.

"I have come to accept that doing the kind of work I do can be alienating. I see it in my own circles. It is very difficult for people to put aside fears and judgments and engage with people they know very little about or with whom they disagree."

"Who cares if we disagree?" I complain. "Is it really our job to exclude and judge based on something we believe is wrong? Why can't we just let God be the judge and all work together when it comes to saving lives?"

We turn left, away from the harbor and back toward

Grant Park. Music is blaring from a boom box on a grassy lawn. A dance troupe of gay men dressed in army fatigues are performing as the walkers move past. Brad says, "Did you know Quakers have guidelines for communication? The most important guideline is that we all be willing to be convinced, but not try to convince others. This openness to change has to come from a place of quiet. We aren't asked to sacrifice our individual values, but we are pushed to open our eyes, heart, and mind to see common ground where we may not have seen it before. It is challenging, but something Quakers have valued for over 350 years."

As always, I am feeling challenged by Brad. "You know, I often feel like I'm in no-man's-land," I confess. "My faith community—well, nobody really knows what to do with me. I am a suburban mom. I don't work for anyone. I have no title. Liberals would laugh if I considered myself liberal, and conservatives won't really own me either. I'm just sort of out here on my own."

Brad shrugs, "Is that such a bad thing? For years I felt a similar way until it occurred to me, maybe no-man's-land is a real place, not simply a place of limbo. In fact, maybe it is a position of real power and influence."

The nerve endings in my soul are firing again.

He muses, "Maybe it is from these places of in-between where we can learn from each other and practice engaging in dialogue that is led by love."

- Approximately 56,300 new HIV infections occurred in the United States in 2006. This number is approximately 40 percent higher than the CDC's previous estimate of 40,000 new infections per year.[1]
- Although the new estimates illustrate the challenges of fighting HIV, there is significant evidence that prevention can — and does — work when we apply what we know.[2]
- The incidence in the U.S. of contracting HIV: 57 percent is male-to-male sexual contact, 31 percent is high-risk heterosexual contact, and 12 percent is injection drug use.[3]

SUDDENLY TOO REAL

The complaint was the answer. To have heard myself making it was to be answered.... I saw well why the gods do not speak to us openly, nor let us answer. Till that word can be dug out of us, why should they hear the babble we think we mean? How can they meet us face to face till we have faces?

C. S. Lewis, Till We Have Faces

HONDURAS, 2005

I am starting to panic. What seemed like a good idea no longer does. For the past several minutes, we have been circling over mountains and steep valleys, and I cannot imagine how or where this plane is going to land. We buzz above mountainside after mountainside covered by shanties — cities of scrap metal, broken wooden boards, and plastic tarps thrown together.

"Do you see those mountains over there?" Jim Sells, a therapist and professor with whom I am traveling, asks me. "See how they are bare compared with the other mountainsides? When hurricane Mitch came through, whole mountainsides slid into the valleys and river below, taking homes and people with it." He demonstrates the mass sliding with both his hands. "There was a tremendous loss of life — almost 11,000 people died in that hurricane. It is the second deadliest hurricane on record."

I shudder as I look down and involuntarily picture what a pile of homes and humans would look like. I have no category in my brain for this kind of tragedy. I see a landing strip come into view and a larger valley, complete with the instantly recognizable signs of a Pizza Hut and a McDonald's. We are landing in Tegucigalpa, Honduras, a city I did not know existed a few months ago.

As with much of my awakening to the realities of our

global family, I am bothered by my ignorance. When I was invited to travel to Honduras with a group of grant writers and doctors, I knew nothing about the country. I had *heard* of Honduras, certainly, and I knew people who had traveled to the country for short-term mission trips. But when they mentioned the capital city, Tegucigalpa, it was like a foreign word. How could I know nothing about a city of more than 1.2 million people in my own hemisphere?

At the airport, Dr. Enoch Padilla, our host for the next four days, greets us. Our group of grant writers and professors from Northern Illinois University plan to see the work he is doing with HIV and AIDS in the Honduran capital and to explore the idea of creating an NFP (not-for-profit organization) to help support Dr. Padilla's clinic.

At the outskirts of the city, we make a sharp turn in the SUV and start a steep climb up the side of a mountain. I am alarmed enough to let out a small cry when we come to a screeching halt at a traffic jam caused by too many cars trying to merge onto one very small road. My head whips forward, and when it returns to its upright position, out my open window I am face-to-face with a group of men loudly discussing their weapons. There is some silent panic praying on my part and disapproving grunts on their part. I turn to stare at the seat in front of me, as if to say, "I see this every day. Carry on."

"I hope you are not too tired," Dr. Padilla says. "I want to take you to see a client and her family right now. I told them you would come. They are expecting us." Our host turns off the paved road onto a very rough dirt road with deep ruts. I put the window up to hide from the dust storm we are creating.

We are in a slum—a colorful, crazy, filthy teeming-with-life slum.

My heart is always a little too close to the surface, and I can feel a complaint of my soul rise in tears. I have never seen anything like this in real life. Too many people are in too many places doing too many things at once. Walking, sitting, sleeping, eating, sweeping, running, playing, screaming. It is a rude shock to my Western sensibilities. We are not driving by homes! We are passing makeshift tents held up by branches, broomsticks, and rickety boards. Children are barely clothed and are filthy. And it smells. I have never experienced firsthand this kind of poverty; these people are living in worse conditions than our animals do in the U.S.

The car continues to climb up and up and up the ragged dirt road. I stare out the window and think, *Does this place end?* I am starting to feel panic at the seemingly endless mass of people, dust, dogs, and dirt. My heart incredulously demands to God, *Where ARE you? Are you here? You have to be here!*

At that moment two things happen.

First, a white butterfly flutters and hovers at my window. That might not mean anything to you, but God and I have this thing with butterflies. It actually started with Juleen, for whom God consistently shows up in the presence of white butterflies. This ongoing narrative in our friendship and in her spiritual life is a well-known and well-loved story.

Second, a little girl, maybe five years old, runs in front of our car. Her dirty bare feet and scrawny legs flit by as she flies her kite — her kite that is a stick above her head with a plastic bag tied to the tip. She is laughing, and she is being followed by a white butterfly. I watch this little girl and her kite as long as I can before we jerk to the right and come to a stop.

Both of these gestures, it would seem, should have been enough to calm my indignant, affronted soul. But I was too far into my complaint against God with the situation of the slum, and even though I saw the butterflies and I knew full well their meaning, my rebellious heart chose to dismiss them.

We crawl, bumped and bruised, out of the car. I am thankful we have stopped at a home that seems somewhat substantial compared to most others we passed. We walk up cement stairs and enter one large room, which serves as the family's living room, kitchen, and bedrooms. The walls are painted a bright robin's egg blue; in one corner stands a refrigerator and one small burner. A green plastic tub serves as the kitchen sink.

Dr. Padilla, interpreting, introduces us to Rose and to her husband and children. He explains Rose is HIV positive and two of her four children also have the virus. There are two pictures on the walls. One is a large framed poster of the classic Catholic image of the Last Supper. The other is a family photograph. It takes me several minutes to realize the picture on the wall is of this family. I compare the healthy, plump people in the photograph with the sallow, sad people in this room. I breathe deep, trying to control myself. The poverty and disease here are making me angry. I do not want to have to deal with this.

Dr. Padilla invites us to sit down as he and Rose visit. I want to be professional and nod at all the right times. I have been on my journey of global awareness and advocacy with HIV/AIDS and poverty for a few years now. I have read books, gone to meetings, joined the ONE Campaign, hosted events, and championed letter-writing campaigns to Congress.

Then I turn my head and watch the oldest daughter quietly begin preparing the family supper, the oldest daughter who is also HIV positive and not on medication, and the tidal wave of the crisis bears down and almost drowns me. My anger instantly turns to overwhelming sadness.

I cannot contain my tears, and I am starting to feel uneasy and trapped by my unwieldy emotions. Jim glances over at me. I can tell he is reading me, and he steps closer in an almost protective gesture.

I am feeling exposed and I excuse myself, claiming I want to go to the car and get my camera. Dr. Padilla hands me the keys and I bolt out the door. I am thankful night has fallen. Feeling raw and exposed, I welcome the darkness to hide me in this horrible, strange place. The road has cleared of people. Alone, I weep, held up by the side of the dusty SUV.

I pray. I need to pull it together. I need to set these emotions to the side. I will deal with them later. I do not want to be rude or make this lovely family feel bad. I grab my camera and take some deep breaths. As I reenter the room, Dr. Padilla is explaining that Rose is an important member of Solidaridad & Vida, the name of the AIDS clinic. Rose helps facilitate a weekly support group for people living with HIV. She also is a member of the women's micro-finance project.

Although her husband contracted the disease before Rose, Rose's illness has progressed to AIDS while her husband is still only HIV positive. Today Rose is very sick. I glance at the photo on the wall and the tidal wave rears again. The face in the frame is of a beautifully plump wife and mother. In stark contrast, the woman in front of me is thin with sallow cheeks and very sad eyes.

Then it hits me.

The husband … He … Had … It … First.

Which means he brought the killer virus to his wife, who then gave birth to two children who also contracted the disease. He had it first. He slept with someone other than his wife, maybe a prostitute who was HIV positive, and he brought death to his home. This is the achingly common narrative in the developing world, but in this moment, that statistic is enfleshed in Rose. Grief, anger, and profound sadness create a whirling dervish in my soul. All I can think is, *This is genocide by promiscuity!*

I grip the seat of my aluminum folding chair, hoping it might ground me and keep me from flying off into hysterical crying. I keep my eyes down, not able to look at the family the rest of the evening. It is too painful. Everything I have learned about HIV and AIDS is suddenly too real.

●

I see Rose again a few days later. We are attending a support group for people living with HIV and AIDS. Programs working with people living with this disease take a holistic approach, focusing not only on prevention or treatment but also on many things that contribute to the crisis and the well-being of people who are sick, such as nutrition, access to clean water, vocational support, and spiritual and emotional care.

I have had time to process the things I have seen, and today I am in control of my emotions. Yet a tinge of anger toward God remains. I am finding it hard to see how he would allow people to live in these conditions, to have these lives and these problems. I know him as a loving God. I do not doubt him or his love for me, but I am having a hard time transferring my experiences and knowledge of him to this place where people are suffering greatly and, quite frankly, I am feeling betrayed by him. I want to believe my God would not allow these things.

In an inner courtyard of the Solidaridad & Vida clinic, we set up chairs in a circle and greet the women as they enter. Only one man is present today, and I wonder if this is the norm.

Dr. Padilla interprets for us here and there, but mostly we simply observe. Even without help from Dr. Padilla, it is clear Rose is struggling today. When tears aren't streaming down her face, she speaks in short, monotone sentences. The meeting ends, and I notice Rose with a group of ladies visiting in a corner of the courtyard. I watch them for a time, confronted with my own feelings of helplessness and despair. But something stirs inside me. Maybe the habit of hope?

Feeling brave, I ask, "Would it be okay to ask if they would like to pray together? I would like to pray for Rose."

Dr. Padilla interprets my request.

The women's eyes light up at the suggestion, and we quickly form a smaller version of the circle of chairs. My English and their Spanish flow naturally back and forth, and we take turns as if in a conversation. We all seem confident the Spirit is communicating despite our language barrier.

With my head bowed and listening to the Spanish prayers, I think, *How am I here? Two days ago I was in the carpool lane at my son's preschool and hurrying home to throw something together for dinner, but today I am in Honduras with strangers who have tragic and serious problems. Yet we are praying as if with friends.*

"Usted es un angel." Rose grabs my face after we say amen. She is glowing with happiness. She keeps repeating this and talking in hurried Spanish, her glowing eyes full of tears. I smile back with matching tears and beg someone to interpret as she keeps talking and holding my face.

"She says you are an angel," replies one of the clinic workers. "She says you were sent to comfort her. She is thanking you for coming and for caring. She knows you will take her story and her sorrows back to people who can help. She says you are an angel."

I gasp, chills running from my scalp to my toes. I have been angry and arguing with God for days and *she thinks I am an angel*?

Almost involuntarily, I reach up and touch her face. And mostly to myself, I murmur, "God bless you, Rose. He *does* love you. He really does." Beneath my fingers I feel the warmth of her skin and the wet of her tears—my reaching out and Rose receiving the touch transfers divine grace to us both—a language we both understand.

- Around the world, over 1 billion people survive on less than a dollar a day.[1]
- Around the world, one person in seven goes to bed hungry each night.[2]
- Women bear the brunt of global poverty and disease. Women work longer hours earning less money, face fewer educational and political opportunities, and are more vulnerable to HIV than their male counterparts.[3]

8

JESUS AT THE G8[1]

It is this movement of church people and trade unionists, soccer moms and student activists that will carry the spirit of Live 8 on. It is this movement, not rock stars, which will make it untenable in the future for world leaders to break promises to the most vulnerable people on this planet.

Bono, 2005

EDINBURGH, SCOTLAND, 2005

"Tatia, that's the same thing he had on yesterday!" I exclaim to my traveling friend and fellow ONE Campaign delegate.

Bob Geldof is dressed in what look like linen pajamas that seem to have been crumpled up on the bottom of his closet for a year. He climbs to stand on one of the chairs in the sectioned-off area of Heathrow. I smirk, thinking, *I suppose his celebrity-ness needed to be shielded from the average traveler.*

It had been over twenty-four hours since I had seen Bob Geldof on the JumboTron screen. I was in Philadelphia with front-row seats to the Live 8 concert, and he was on stage at the show in Hyde Park, in London. Now standing about ten feet from him, I can clearly see he has not slept, showered, or changed his clothes since then.

He raises his hands and accepts our applause. I cannot stop laughing. He is scruffy and disheveled, yet I am smitten with this concert organizer/rocker turned awareness raiser.

As a result of my work with ONE and World Vision and other local advocacy efforts, I was invited to attend the G8 Summit in Edinburgh, Scotland, as a delegate for the ONE Campaign — the Campaign to Make Poverty History. We traveled to Philadelphia to attend the Live 8 Concert, one of a dozen free concert events held around the world. Live 8 was a huge outdoor concert on July 2, 2005, in Philadelphia, with corresponding concerts held in places like London, Paris, Berlin, and Rome—all timed to precede the G8 Summit in Scotland to raise global awareness and to pressure world leaders to drop the debt of the world's poorest nations, increase and improve aid, and negotiate fair trade rules in the interest of poorer countries.

There are about a hundred delegates from our Philadelphia flight crammed into this waiting area. "Richard and I are so thankful for you all. You are the heart of this movement!" We cheer. Bob gestures to Richard Branson, who is standing next to him. Richard Branson is a British billionaire who was knighted by the Queen of England. He is owner of Virgin Records and Virgin Atlantic Airlines.

Bob puts his arm around Richard. "We can get attention, but it's going to take everyone to make real change, to make history. We are not looking for charity, we are looking for justice. The G8 world leaders cannot ignore all of us coming together in solidarity with the poor. This is the starting point for the long walk to justice, the one way we can all make our voices heard in unison."

Bob Geldof is a former singer with the rock band Boomtown Rats, a band I have to admit I know very little about, as I am wholly illiterate of the 1970s Irish rock scene. He is also famous for organizing the Live Aid concert of twenty years ago, which opened the eyes of a generation in America and Europe to the harsh reality of daily life and death in Africa. That concert's goal was to raise money for Africa, but the Live 8 concert series has a different goal: to raise awareness and to fight for justice when it comes to global poverty.

"We're all here!" Bob Geldof shouts enthusiastically. "We finally got here, the gathering of clans from all over the world, from all over Scotland and the U.K. We told the world leaders we'd come!"

Loud shouts and cheers fill the small space, and I smile as Richard Branson says, "It is my honor to fly this fine delegation from London to Edinburgh in a few hours and personally deliver you to the G8 Summit."

●

"Would you like some champagne?" the Virgin Atlantic supermodel flight attendant asks politely.

"Thank you." I chuckle. "Tatia, we have landed on another planet."

"You mean we're flying to another planet?" We both look around wide-eyed and very amused.

We were on a party plane headed for the G8 Summit, complete with loud music, people milling around sipping champagne, celebrities talking with the press, and the press wondering how all these people with ONE T-shirts got on this plane — all with owner and consummate host, Richard Branson, presiding over the whole thing.

"Shayne, is that George Clooney?" Tatia snorts on her champagne.

"No. That is *not* him, but I've heard he is going to be at the G8 Summit as a celebrity ONE delegate."

Tatia is a lawyer in Chicago and full-time mother, and our paths cross often in our advocacy work. I am so thankful to have her with me because this is all new territory.

Tatia and I settle into our seats and get out our media

briefing booklets. As ONE delegates, we will be doing interviews with the national and international press. Not only do we need to know the facts of various issues, we need to be able to articulate them clearly in an interview. Neither of us has done anything like this before, so we practice with each other, although the several glasses of complimentary champagne don't seem to be helping.

My learning curve is precipitous. A few weeks ago I didn't even know what the G8 Summit was or why it was so important. The G8 is an entity known as the "Group of Eight"—eight of the world's leading nations. The leaders of these countries meet face-to-face once a year. The organization, formed in 1975 as the Group of Six (G6), brought together six nations to focus on the global economic and oil crisis of that time. Canada joined in 1976, Russia in 1997. Today the G8 Summit also focuses on issues such as the developing world, global security, Middle East peace, and reconstruction in Iraq.

The leaders of France, Germany, Italy, Japan, Britain, the United States, Canada, and Russia meet to agree on global policies and to set objectives. The country holding the presidency of the G8 in any given year is responsible for hosting the annual summit. This year, Prime Minister Tony Blair of Great Britain is the president and host of the G8, and he has put the humanitarian crisis in Africa on the agenda. Taking advantage of this, activists are using the opportunity to raise awareness with slogans, celebrities, politicians, and concerts.

Tatia looks at the seat in front of her and recites, "ONE is a new effort by Americans to rally Americans—ONE by ONE — to fight the emergency of global AIDS and extreme poverty. ONE is students, ministers, punk rockers, soccer moms ..." Tatia starts to giggle and pokes me. "That's you!"

"I'm pretty sure I'm not the only soccer mom in the ONE Campaign. C'mon, focus," I tease back.

Sitting up straighter, she recites, "ONE believes that allocating an additional ONE percent to the U.S. budget toward providing basic needs like health, education, clean water, and food would transform the futures and hopes of an entire generation in the world's poorest countries. ONE also calls for debt cancellation, trade reform, and anticorruption measures in a comprehensive package to help Africa and the poorest nations beat AIDS and extreme poverty."

"Very impressive." I smile. "It's one thing to know all this and another to be able to say it concisely and under pressure to the press. Okay, my turn."

I turn over my media briefing book and say to the tray table in front of me, "Most Americans would be surprised to learn that less than 1 percent of the federal budget is currently marked for development assistance. If the U.S. were to devote an additional ONE percent — one cent for every dollar spent by the federal government — to helping the world's poorest people help themselves, America would demonstrate a commitment to the Millennium Development Goals, an internationally agreed upon effort to halve global poverty by 2015."

"Whoo-hoo!" Tatia says. "You nailed it, but don't forget to get in the stuff about how many lives will be saved — with an additional 1 percent of our budget we can help prevent 10 million children from becoming AIDS orphans, we can help get 104 million children into grade school, we can help provide clean water to almost 900 million people around the globe, and save almost 6.5 million children under five from dying of diseases that could be prevented with low-cost measures like vaccination or a well for clean water."

I look at Tatia. "Um, you were just reading all that. I'm not sure we're gonna have a cheat sheet to remember all those statistics."

"I know," Tatia moans, "but the statistics are so important. They say so much!"

We read silently and memorize until we're interrupted.

"Can you believe this?" Amy is making her way back to her seat from some power networking in the aisles of the plane. Amy and I got to know each other a bit during the few days we spent in Philadelphia.

"No, I cannot believe this." I shake my head and smile ear to ear.

Amy leans her arm on the seat in front of me. "I fully expected to be traveling with others like me — liberal, socially aware Democrats. I didn't expect ONE delegates to include so many Christians like you. I can't believe the range of interests, faith backgrounds, and ages among this group of people — yet we still are managing to speak with one voice."

Amy looks around the plane and exclaims, "I've never seen anything like it!" Then, looking back at me, she says, "And you, you're the real surprise to me."

As members of the delegation to the G8 Summit, we

had received a press booklet that included talking points and brief biographies of the delegates on the trip. With so much travel time, we had all gotten a chance to familiarize ourselves with one another. My bio included a description of me as an "evangelical soccer mom."

I join in on the enthusiasm, but I'm not sure if I should feel complimented or offended. "I couldn't agree more. All these different people coming together, it is very inspiring. But you crack me up. Why do I surprise you? C'mon, socially conscious Christian moms are not that obscure, are we?" I laugh while Amy and Tatia each make a face.

Internally I had to agree with the raised eyebrows and silence. There was no one else here like me. I have no background in political activism or social policy. I got involved because I went to hear Bono, but I stay involved because now I cannot turn away from the realities of preventable death and poverty. From where I sat — namely, inside my own self — it seemed completely natural and logical that a Christian mother from Middle America would care about the humanitarian crisis in Africa. But from where my seatmates sat, I was an aberration.

"So, tell me, Shayne, what do you do back home — I mean, are you just a mom?" This is Amy making small talk.

I smile and try to stay cordial. "Ah, I'm certainly more than *just* a mom, but that is my primary job right now."

"That's great," she says unconvincingly. "I think it's really incredible you are here. I never expected to see an evangelical here — especially a soccer mom. This kind of stuff never interests them."

Dodging the second dig at my mom status, I answer, somewhat defensively, "Amy, if you look at demographics, conservative Christians are some of the most generous with our time, our volunteerism, and our money. I truly believe if people are informed and educated, they will act."

"Perhaps, but why is it taking so long to inform in certain Christian circles around these issues? Is it prejudice? Political belief?"

I sigh. "I don't know. I think it's a mixture of a lot of things. Sadly, maybe it does include issues of prejudice, misinformation, and political leanings—some feel threatened that engaging with all this is something only liberals do. It's hard to convince people they do not need to change their faith or political convictions in order to get involved." Amy does not seem to soften. I add, "I admit, I have been frustrated with my faith tradition, but I truly believe it is just a matter of time."

Amy gives me a smile tinted with patronization. "You are very gracious with your community."

Getting a bit more heated, I say, "It's because I am gracious with myself. Look, I had to learn all of this from step one. I had no one around to teach me or guide me—especially as a stay-at-home mom. But I kept going because of my faith in a loving God who is deeply grieved by what is happening to the poor.

"Amy"—I bring the tone down a bit—"I believe when Christian women are informed, their faith will compel them to action. We believe in a loving Creator who works in our world through us. I say, then let's act like it! Let's inform ourselves of what is going on in our world and in our generation and make a difference."

Is this a moment we're having?

"You bring me hope, Shayne"—and here Amy pats me on the shoulder, like she would a child, and the moment disintegrates like a popped soap bubble—"you're so cute." She moves on down the aisle toward her next glass of champagne.

This is the 935th time I have realized that I am not a part of the club. I have not been trained in public policy, I know very little about international and foreign relations, I am not a journalist, and I do not work for a not-for-profit organization or a ministry. And what I am—a suburban Christian mother—tells most people all they need to know about me. I don't appreciate what this says about me; I loathe what this says about my faith tradition.

Many of the delegates I met work for some of the nonprofit organizations that partner with ONE, such as CARE, DATA, International Medical Corps, Oxfam America, and World Vision. Since I wear no official hat, people don't really know what to do with me, the "soccer mom." In nearly every circle—from family to church to community to globally—I seem to be an enigma. People don't seem to know how to interact with me, understand where my sphere of influence might be, or grasp why in the world I am interested or involved.

Early in our life together, my husband and I made a decision I would stay home as we grew our family. It was a scary sacrifice at the time—to rely on one income—but I felt blessed with the opportunity, knowing not all women who want to stay home with their babies are able to. Yet, over time I came to realize the decision to stay home had made my world very small. I moved in a very insular circle of friends, family, and church. For instance, I did not have opportunities to interact with work colleagues who might be wildly different from me. I lived and moved in a very homogeneous bubble.

As I head to Edinburgh, I am aware that I am the only self-identifying evangelical Christian woman in this delegation. There are other Christians here. I met pastors and lay leaders who attend mainline Protestant or Catholic churches, but I have not met another conservative Christian like me. This led me to the uncomfortable discovery that people do not think highly of evangelicals outside of evangelical circles. It's sort of a dirty word, to be honest. At the mere mention of it, a slew of assumptions, opinions, and ideologies are placed on me—an experience that has helped me understand at least one reason why evangelicals aren't well regarded.

This labeling and prejudice bother me, and Amy's attitude is another confirmation that my status as "evangelical soccer mom" puts me at the bottom of the activist heap.

I give up trying to focus on the media training booklet. I am disheartened and think about my friend Brad and about Rose in Honduras. I turn to look out the plane window, reflecting on what I have seen and learned these past few years.

I wonder, *Why do people need to label? It is not useful and only divides.*

But this interaction with Amy strikes a deeper chord in

me. In the church where I grew up, being a woman means I am barred from being a pastor, a deacon, or an elder. I cannot hold a place of authority within the leadership of a church. I have listened to sermons where I was told, as a woman, I have no say in the vision or guidance of a congregation. I am to submit to the male leadership of my church — no questions asked.

One thing I did "outside the home" while my kids were very young was to go back to school. Taking one class at a time, I slowly received a master of arts in theology. I worked hard, and it was not easy to take classes, study, and write papers while I had toddlers. I was proud of myself for completing it. But I have often reflected on the fact that no one around me really noticed or cared about the accomplishment. Where I come from, the stay-at-home-mom title is the highest calling and brings the highest respect.

I have friends and family members who do not understand what I am doing, traveling around the world and leaving my family for these causes. How many times have I arranged meetings with various missions' pastors and community outreach pastors with naïve hopes they will catch a vision for this movement? But the reality is, coming from a woman in my faith tradition — well, it just doesn't carry a lot of weight.

I love being a stay-at-home mom. I love that it is *me* who deals with the chaos of early mornings before school — packing lunches, making sure everyone has backpacks ready and the appropriate coat on. I love that it is *me* who reads, does puzzles, referees sibling quarrels, and makes dinner every night. But what I don't love is that my job as a stay-at-home limits me—in my church and in the world. I don't understand why it can't be "both/and." I don't understand why it is such a struggle—to do what I love, which is to take care of my family *and* to have a voice in my church and make a difference in my world.

I treasure the opportunity to be a stay-at-home mom, and I cherish my faith tradition. It is my family. It has been passed to me through many generations from my mother and my father. I resonate deeply with the emphasis on the Word of God, on the Trinitarian God, on Christ's resurrection, and on God's ultimate plan to heal creation. As I followed God's call to have a heart for the poor and oppressed and then the desire to *do* something about it, I started by approaching my faith tradition. I would have loved to have journeyed this in the safety of my faith family. But the reality is, I had to go outside my tradition to keep moving on this journey of engaging issues of global social justice.

Not only this, I have also been hit hard by outside opinions of the status of full-time mothers. In this strange place of movers and shakers, celebrities and socially active liberals and lobbyists, this very thing—my identity as mother—which gives me more credibility than an advanced degree or passion or intelligence in my community, is the very thing that makes me so "cute."

I can no longer engage in the party atmosphere of Richard Branson's plane as I feel the pinch between these two worlds. I feel resentful and discouraged.

●

Roxy Art House was once a church in Edinburgh, Scotland.

As Christianity declined in Europe, many churches were left vacant or, as in this case, recycled. Today Roxy Art House is part coffeehouse and part café. It is used as a concert venue for Scottish artists and as an art studio. The high ceilings, ornate arches, carved stone walls, and stained glass window depicting Christ's passion story are all intact. This week, the week of the historic G8 Summit, Roxy Art House is ONE Campaign headquarters.

Gathered in Edinburgh are 250,000 people from around the world. Places like Britain and Japan also have campaigns similar to ONE. We are just the American delegation,[2] and all of us, as a global community, are asking world leaders to double financial aid to the world's poorest countries, to cancel the debt for the poorest nations, and to reform trade laws so poor nations are not shut out of global markets.

The ONE staff hands out cell phones to us and instructs us to be available for interviews at a moment's notice. We will gather at Roxy Art House for meetings and briefings and for the staff to organize us.

"Tatia, I am so tired, I am about to fall over." I slump in my chair and collapse on the table. We are two days into the summit. Two days of crowds, interviews, meetings, and jet lag.

"So much drama, Shayne." Tatia sips her umpteenth cup of coffee. "I am really wiped out too, but they said, 'Don't leave.' I do what I'm told."

Even though it is only mid-afternoon, I feel as if it were midnight. "I think these political campaigners are insane.

They never stop working. Either that or they are trying to kill us."

The whole world seems to have their eyes on this G8 Summit, and everybody is taking advantage of the world's focus. Anarchist protestors have taken to the streets in Edinburgh to protest. To be honest, I am not really sure what they are protesting. I suppose I am here protesting in my own way—playing my role in getting the ONE message out in interviews with places like WGN (my radio station back home), TV network CBN, and with magazines such as *Good News* and *Christianity Today*.

Finally a commotion. I do a double-take as the people at the crowded tables come to attention. George Clooney is being escorted to the nave of Roxy Art House.

I smile at Tatia. "I'm awake now."

We cheer loudly for our counterpart celebrity delegate. "Greetings, fellow ONE delegates," George Clooney says to the crowd. "It's pretty incredible what is happening in this city, in the world, this week, no? Wow. And all of you." He gestures at us.

We, of course, cheer for ourselves.

George positions himself on a stool and settles in. "I am truly honored to be here with ONE and honored to be associated with this amazing group of delegates. I hear you all have been busy. I want to thank you for all your hard work, both here this week and all you do back in your hometowns."

I am smiling and a bit dazed and think, *He is much shorter than I expected.*

George Clooney is dressed in a blue polo shirt and a

brown blazer. He looks very normal and about as tired as the rest of us.

He continues. "As a celebrity, I can draw media attention, use my celebrity as currency, if you will, and spend it on behalf of those who might never get this kind of voice. We have a historic opportunity this week to communicate to the eight most powerful nations that the world cares about what is happening to the least of these, to the poorest of the poor in our world.

"The G8 leaders must make strong commitments to reaching the Millennium Development Goals by 2015. This generation may be the first generation in history to have the resources to end extreme poverty—to end the fact that four times the population of the entire United States live on less than a dollar a day."

As a part of the education of Shayne Moore, I have also learned about the Millennium Development Goals, or MDGs. In 2000, world leaders at the United Nations committed to a set of development goals to alleviate extreme global poverty. The leaders of 189 countries, including the United States, committed themselves to implementing a set of goals known as MDGs. These countries pledged to "spare no effort to free our fellow men, women, and children from the abject and dehumanizing conditions of extreme poverty."

The reason this G8 Summit is so important is because Tony Blair, the prime minister of Great Britain and current president of the G8, put Africa and the MDGs on the agenda. Five years after the Millennium Summit, when these goals were first made, the world is still decades behind in meeting them. The World Bank and the United Nations have estimated that an additional $40 billion to $60 billion will be needed globally every year until 2015 to achieve the MDGs.[3]

At this G8 Summit, ONE is asking that 100 percent of multilateral debt be dropped for impoverished nations — nineteen in all — of HIPC (Heavily Indebted Poor Countries). I was unaware of this before getting involved, but many nations are still paying debt from several generations ago — debt incurred by corrupt regimes. These impoverished nations have no chance of getting on the global economic ladder without full debt cancellation. In the world's most impoverished nations, the majority of the populations do not have access to clean water or basic health care. These poor nations are paying their debt to wealthy nations at the expense of providing basic needs to their citizens. Also, some poor countries pay more in debt than they receive in aid. I know I'm no expert, but this seems upside down.

Having seen firsthand the slums of Tegucigalpa in Honduras and after meeting Rose and her family, all this global social policy talk means something to me. These are real people in a real place who are really suffering. And by relieving the debt of the poorest nations, including Honduras, the world community can move forward in achieving the Millennium Development Goals. Resources can be redirected to help the people.

These are the Millennium Development Goals set by the United Nations in 2000:

1. Eradicate extreme poverty and hunger.

2. Achieve universal primary education.
3. Promote gender equality and empower women.
4. Reduce child mortality.
5. Improve maternal health.
6. Combat HIV/AIDS, malaria, and other diseases.
7. Ensure environmental sustainability.
8. Develop a global partnership for development.

"In 2000 the world made a commitment," George Clooney tells us. "The world embraced a vision. The most powerful nations are behind on these commitments, but the world's voices, our voices, are here in Edinburgh, Scotland, to tell them they must keep their promises to the world's poorest people."

There is a quiet, sincere passion about George Clooney, and I like it.

His eyes sparkle as he says, "As our friend and fearless leader, Bono, often says, 'We have the global resources to end stupid poverty, but do we have the political will?'"

As George says this, the sun comes out from behind a cloud in Edinburgh. An alcove of the nave of what was once a church bursts full of color and lights up behind him. The stained glass windows that once crowned an altar come to life, and a single beam of light from the halo above an image of Christ beams down directly on top of his head.

- Halfway to the target date of 2010, the G8 has delivered only a third of its promises of aid to sub-Saharan Africa.[4]
- In Tanzania, savings from debt cancellations helped the government abolish primary school fees, leading to 3.1 million children now in school.[5]
- Mozambique used its debt relief savings to vaccinate children against tetanus, whooping cough, and diphtheria, as well as to install electricity in schools and to build new schools.[6]
- Debt cancellation has saved African countries $93 billion since 1996, which, along with targeted aid for education, helped send 34 million more African children to school for the first time.[7]
- In 2000, leaders from 189 countries signed on to the Millennium Development Goals (MDGs), a set of eight ambitious targets designed to significantly reduce global poverty and disease by 2015.[8]
- Tangible results prove that dramatic progress is possible when developing countries and donor governments fulfill their commitments.[9]
- Increased global resources for health have helped an estimated 4 million HIV-positive people receive lifesaving ARV medication.[10]

9

A HOPE-SHAPED ACHE

It was a strongly held belief of most first-century Jews, and virtually all early Christians, that history was going somewhere under the guidance of God and that where it was going was toward God's new world of justice, healing, and hope. The transition from the present world to the new one would be a matter not of the destruction of the present space-time universe but of its radical healing.

N. T. Wright, Surprised by Hope

Kenya, 2005

Every night they gather to sing. For an hour before bedtime, the orphans on the other side of the hedge sing praise songs to God. There are sixty-six orphans living in the orphanage next to our guesthouse in Litien, Kenya.

Walking back to my room, I am stopped in my tracks by the perfectly pitched, hauntingly beautiful voices of children. They sing in Swahili and in English. The volume is sometimes loud and boisterous and joyful. At times the children sing with a peaceful quiet, full of reverence. It is pitch dark on this far-flung hillside in Kenya. I stand alone, wishing the mesmerizing music would stop. *What is this ache in my heart?* It feels almost too much, as if it might crack something foundational in me, something I am quite sure I need intact. Yet I linger, unable to leave it and shut it out. I stare at the hedge that separates us and listen.

I try to remind myself I am simply having a typical response to being confronted by outrageous poverty and inequality. I have tried to categorize it, explain it, critique it, and process it with the other members on my team. Yet my heart is causing me trouble. This is not the first time I have seen firsthand the staggering reality of extreme poverty and the wildly disparate gap between America and the developing world, but it is something I never get used to.

The past few days I have not been able to stop the

frantic tape in my head from playing over and over, asking, *Where is God? How can this be? How can he endure this kind of human suffering? Where is the justice? Where is relief and healing and clean water? Why should our quality of life depend so much on where we're born?*

Last night I had a dream.

I am in a quiet African village in which the people are eking out an impoverished existence. I am following a man. I mysteriously understand he is a God-figure. He is walking in front of me, leading me down the red clay roads. I stumble on the rocky terrain and do my best to keep up with him. He does not speak, a lone figure on the dirty, rough roads. Silently he begins to point things out to me. I watch as he points down an alley. I follow as he points into this house, at that field, toward a distant well. We continue to walk — it seems endlessly — as he purposefully points the way.

Even while still dreaming, a realization comes to me, *He can do something.*

I am filled with an aching hope. Alone I can do nothing or even begin to bring relief to the immense suffering I have seen. I can do nothing to stop the onslaught of AIDS, the exploitation of women and children, the stupid poverty. In my dream, I come to terms with my helplessness. By myself I *am* helpless, but I'm not here by myself. I am not alone — in Africa, in the World, or in my generation with all its troubles — God is here.

I reflect on this dream as the orphans over the hedge finish their nightly praise songs to God. I turn to enter the guesthouse where the team is staying. Flipping on the light in the small kitchen, I stand still, giving the roaches and mice time to jump off the counter and scurry across the cement floor. For the first few days, we tried vigilantly to keep the vermin off our food supply, but we soon gave up. How quickly you learn to accept things it seems you cannot control in this strange place. I boil water to make a cup of tea and cannot keep my mind from reflecting on my visit to the orphanage yesterday.

●

Eight white buildings surround a yard in a square. As we make our way across the compound, I look into the doorless dwellings. The floors of the bunkhouses are cement, and the bunk beds inside them hold thin, mostly bare mattresses except for an occasional blanket. I pause at one door, noticing I see no personal belongings. As I continue on my way I almost run into an emaciated cow lumbering and grazing on the anemic grass lawn.

My mother's heart is aching terribly, and I stepped foot in this orphanage only three minutes ago. Already, I see my three-year-old in a child holding an older boy's hand, my six-year-old daughter giggling with her hand over her mouth, and my ten-year-old son running like a madman, playfully hitting a friend and dodging retribution as he heads toward the multipurpose room where the children are gathering.

In the meeting hall, the children sit in rows on benches, their ill-fitting uniforms stained and ripped. I want to scrub them all down, head to toe, then get them some decent clothes and a good meal. My heart and mind are not happy with this moment and desperately want to slip away to a place where they do not have to deal with this—the impossible longing to give a mother's care to every needy child in the world.

After greeting us, the children sing. It is a gospel song in English, "In paradise, everything is gonna be all right. In paradise everything is gonna be okay, okay, okay." As they sing, they sway back and forth in perfect unison. Back and forth. Back and forth. Everything is going to be okay, left, okay, right, okay, left.

Hypnotic, dull eyes, no smiles. Okay, left, okay, right, okay, left.

Disconcertingly, the swaying speaks to me of self-comfort, self-soothing. How a mother might gather her baby in her arms, rocking and cooing, "It'll be okay, sweetie. It'll be okay." Yet this is an entire room of motherless children soothing themselves.

Can a heart break into a million pieces for the millionth time?

Letting a tear fall down my cheek, I wonder, *Are they going to be okay? What is to become of them? What will their lives look like in two years, five years, ten years? As my children are preparing for college and high school proms, will these children have incurable diseases or abusive husbands? Will they have enough food?*

●

I sip my tea, thankful for creature comforts. Hugging the mug, I put my head back on the ratty cushion of the guesthouse couch. I reflect on this idea that in paradise, everything will be all right. I close my eyes and shake my head in frustration. This kind of theology doesn't cut it for me.

Of course, I believe everything will be made right and all of creation will be redeemed in paradise. When God created the world he said, "It is good." I do not believe God starts over in heaven with a whole new template of creation. This creation, this world, is *good*, and everything good in creation—the beauty of nature, every act of kindness, every gesture of humility and gratitude, every sacrificial offering and deed that builds up the church—all these and more will somehow, mysteriously be continued into the next age. I do not believe when we die we are simply whisked up to heaven to sit on a cloud somewhere. This journey of faith, this world, and each of us—including the orphans over the hedge—we're all going somewhere far more dynamic and meaningful.

I believe this is why God works in this world. He loves this world and he will bring healing. He will make everything right. It is the whole point of the biblical story, that in Jesus' death and resurrection, God broke into humanity and started the world on the course toward full healing.

It is my thinking—and we pray together as Christians—"Thy kingdom come, Thy will be done [on] earth, as it is in heaven" (Matt. 6:9–10 KJV). Jesus himself taught us to pray this way. Jesus didn't say, "Sorry, folks, you'll just have to wait until you get to heaven or until I return for me to work in the world."

Emotionally and psychologically, I understand the temptation to think this way. How quickly did I give up fighting the roaches and mice in my food? It can seem too much. Too overwhelming. What can we really do? If powerful governments and multiple generations before us have not been able to arrest deadly disease, extreme poverty, and the suffering of innocent people, who are we to think we can do any better? I get it, but this acceptance of suffering is not what Jesus taught and it is not God's plan for his creation.

One of my favorite theologians, N. T. Wright, teaches that human beings reflect the image of God, and God intends this reflection of himself to be present in our world, here and now. He has enlisted us to act on his behalf in the project of healing creation and building his kingdom. Because Jesus brought the reality of this healed world through his resurrection, not only is acting on behalf of justice and compassion a way in which we seek God, it is also how we reflect God to a suffering world and build for the kingdom. Wright explains, "You are not planting roses in a garden that's about to be dug up for a building site. You are—strange though it may seem, almost as hard to believe as the resurrection itself—accomplishing something that will become in due course part of God's new world."

Imagine a father and child in the garage, working on building something together. The father knows the plan and could certainly build it himself, but he delights to have his small child with him. He hands the small child a hammer and some nails and some simple instructions. The child does not fully understand the entire project or how it will come together, but she happily starts banging and hammering. The child certainly helps the father, but it is only because the father equipped her. The father delights in including the child because he loves the child and longs to see her participate, but the father alone knows the plan.

First Corinthians 15:58 says, "Always give yourselves fully to the work of the Lord, because you know that your labor in the Lord is not in vain." Ultimately, in paradise, not only does the Father know the plan, but he alone transforms and redeems the whole project. He will "make all things new." Yet we are still called to participate in the healing of creation—that somehow our efforts impact the future, the overall plan, and carry over into paradise.

N. T. Wright explains, "What we do in the Lord is 'not in vain' and that is the mandate we need for every act of justice and mercy, every program of ecology, every effort to reflect God's wise stewardly image into his creation."[1] Creation is to be redeemed. God declared the whole project "very good." This challenges me with the idea of what am I to do in this in-between time—between the resurrection of Jesus and when God makes all things new? As a woman in the church, am I called to just wait in my comfortable life, feeling somewhat bad about the suffering in the world, or am I to work to bring the kingdom of heaven here and now?

●

It just about ripped out my heart to leave all those sad, lifeless orphans in Litien, Kenya, having done nothing to improve their conditions. Yet after our team left Litien, we visited a program of Wheaton Bible Church. We traveled to see a Kenyan woman named Josephine and to observe a feeding and vocational program for the youth in her community.

When we arrived on the site, we entered a meeting hall similar to the one at the orphanage. We were escorted to the front and seated in places of honor. We were fed a humble feast of traditional Kenyan food—ugali (made with cornmeal), greens, a stew with a bit of meat in it, probably goat—aware the entire time the offering of this meal was hugely sacrificial for this poor community.

The children had on uniforms similar to the children in Litien—but these children were different. Their uniforms were clean and their faces were bright and open. These children were struggling to eat and stay in school until Josephine stepped in on behalf of her community. Working with the chiefs of the village, Wheaton Bible Church, and missionaries in Kenya, Josephine developed a program to meet the tangible needs of those around her. Josephine changed her world.

These children, some of them orphans, are loved. It shows as they energetically and joyfully show us their classrooms and their sewing machines, which Wheaton Bible Church helped purchase. I am encouraged that, at least in this place, the eternal reality of healing has begun and it has faces. And the ache inside me begins to fill with hope— that working to meet the needs of suffering people really can change the world.

- Undernutrition contributes to almost half of all child deaths and more than 20 percent of maternal deaths.[2]
- Worldwide, 72 million children, 56 percent of whom are girls, remain out of school.[3]
- Every day, 5,000 children die from severe diarrhea.[4]

10

WHAT IF LOVE RULED THE WORLD?

Global poverty will not be significantly reduced until we forge new international policies and practices regarding aid, trade, and debt while also honestly facing the real issues of governance and transparency in poor countries. Only a new commitment to moral *and* political responsibility on the part of wealthy nations and a new level of public integrity to root out the corruptions that poverty brings in the poor nations will create the capacity for genuine partnerships.

Jim Wallis, God's Politics

Russia, 2006

The room is one small step up from a prison cell. There is a twin bed in the corner, a single lamp, and a rickety night table. The walls are painted stark white with no artwork, but the door has a secure lock, the bathroom is clean, and I cannot remember a time when I have been happier.

I move to the twin windows. There is an iron frame with a deep sill and a crank for opening the windows. I am curious about the antique-y feel of it, and I crank both windows open as far as they will go. The sun is not shining. I stick my head out to see as much as I can. I look left and right and settle back and stare across the rooftops of this strange new place.

I left my family at home and traveled nine time zones to St. Petersburg, Russia, on the Gulf of Finland in the Baltic Sea. The 2006 G8 Summit is being held here. Vladimir Putin is the president of the G8 this year, and for his agenda he has chosen the global issue of infectious disease. However, the wars in Iraq and Afghanistan have overshadowed the 2005 G8 promises of achieving the Millennium Development Goals. There is a much smaller delegation of ONE Campaign members attending the summit. In fact, there is just me. I feel honored and I feel a sense of accomplishment that I made it here.

Knowing the press coverage would be focusing on the

Middle East, ONE has a smaller presence at this year's summit, but with the same goal of getting press attention and urging world leaders to keep their promises to the poorest people on the planet. In 2005, G8 leaders promised $50 billion more in effective international assistance per year by 2010, with half of that for Africa. Some other promises included near universal access to AIDS drugs and care for AIDS orphans and to reduce the impact of malaria by 85 percent and help save the lives of 600,000 children every year.

There is a knock on my door. I have never been in a Communist country before and an unexpected person at my door conjures up images of uniformed KGB coming for me. I open the door, delighted to find Meighan.

Meighan Stone, communications director for ONE, is a superhero. I have never known a woman like Meighan. She could rule the world. In fact, she *should* rule the world. With my involvement with ONE, I have had the great pleasure of watching Meighan in action. She is wildly intelligent, funny, intense, and single-focused, but what I love most about Meighan is that despite the incredible competence with which she does her job, her heart is what is contagious. In my constant search for guides on my journey into global social justice, Meighan Stone is the leader of the pack.

"Hey, lady, are you ready?" Meighan smiles warmly and fusses with one of her many Blackberries.

I hug Meighan, which she receives awkwardly. I chuckle at my nonprofessional status and my mommy ways. I am so happy to see her, a bit of comfort in this unfamiliar place.

Every day I bop from preschool pickup, to grocery store, to post office, to dry cleaners, to home—not from Chicago, to London, to Frankfurt, to Copenhagen, to St. Petersburg.

We make our way to the Neva River to board a ferry that will take us to the G8 Summit in Strelna on the Gulf of Finland, just outside of St. Petersburg. Our commute begins to take on the air of a 1960s spy movie. We are required to stop and pass through several security checkpoints, all of which seem to be held in unfortunate cement, Cold War–era buildings, with uniformed, armed soldiers.

On the ferry, Meighan settles into a seat next to Seth Amgott, communications consultant for the Global Fund to Fight AIDS, TB, and Malaria. They begin chatting and typing away on their respective Blackberries. I do not have a Blackberry and I have never sent a text, though I can pick up toys from the floor of the minivan while driving. Meighan and Seth interact in English, but for all I know they are speaking a foreign language as they discuss forthcoming communiqués and press conferences. I turn to watch the city go by as our ferryboat makes the half-hour commute to Strelna.

St. Petersburg is not at all what I expected. It is a bustling, modern European city with similar architecture to parts of London and Paris. The houses along the Neva River have a baroque feel to them. They are painted soft blues, greens, and even pinks. The trim is white with ornate carvings. Every now and then, a small tributary breaks off this large expressway of a river and meanders under bridges and winds through these delightful structures. The tops of the buildings form a line, as if the architects from days gone by made a pact to build everything only five stories high. As we continue down the river toward the Baltic Sea, from time to time I see the spires of churches go by.

Growing up in the 1970s and 1980s at the end of the Cold War, I pictured Russia as dark and depressing. This city is beautiful. I stare out the window of the ferryboat, willing myself to remember everything I am seeing. I am a long way from Main Street, and I want to take this home with me.

"Shayne, how are you doing? I know you had a brutal trip to get over here, but I am so grateful you made the effort." Meighan dotes as we prepare to disembark. "I am so devastated you got stuck at JFK. I was on the phone with the airline to see if I could move you along or get you on another flight. I really tried. It just didn't happen."

I respond good-naturedly. "It was very disappointing to miss seeing Laura Bush, but I am so glad to be here."

Of *course* Meighan was on the phone with JFK and the airline. Because that is what Meighan does. When this woman has a plan, I do not think anything can stand in her way. Well, except maybe for international flight delays.

I was home on the corner of Main and Front streets just a couple days ago when I received a cell phone call.

"Shayne, it's Meighan." She was speaking in a purposeful tone that was always my cue to listen and follow directions. Meighan has an intelligence that flies at the speed of light. I have learned from our other various projects for ONE to not ask too many questions and to trust her genius.

"We have a tremendous opportunity for you." She was speaking in mover-and-shaker mode. "First Lady Laura

Bush will be touring an AIDS orphanage outside of St. Petersburg on Thursday. I cleared you through her office and you are going to accompany her."

"Really?" The crosswalk light changed, but I did not move. "Wow! This is great news."

"The only thing you need to do is catch a plane in about three hours. Do you think you can make this happen," Meighan asked me in the form of a statement.

"Yes, just tell me what to do. I am already packed, but I was wondering should I try to fit everything into a carry-on?"

"Absolutely." Meighan responded in a tone which was a bit parental and tinged with how-does-someone-not-know-how-to-pack-for-a-G8-Summit?

She added, "Repack ... oh, and pack a suit to meet the First Lady. I'll email your flight information. Call me when you get to the airport."

The light changed again and my adrenaline and mind raced. Repack. Flight in a few hours. The First Lady. I need a suit? And my family — I have a family. I was bemused at how this detail seemed inconsequential to Meighan. I was in a panic trying to figure out how I could leave in a couple of hours and get everyone organized. I had planned to grocery shop and fill up the fridge and pantry before I left.

My husband was very helpful in getting me out the door that day. As I repacked and flung clothes around the room, he sat on the bed and took notes on what still needed to be done.

"Don't forget Greta has orchestra before school on Friday.

"Remember John David's lacrosse stuff is in the trunk.

"Thomas's soccer jersey is in the washer and he has a game on Saturday.

"Tuesday there is a meeting with Thomas's speech teacher.

"Have your mom grocery shop and tell her the kids need protein at breakfast."

There were two-and-a-half more pages.

As it turned out, after all the hurrying, I was forced to wait on the tarmac of a very delayed and crowded JFK airport and missed my connecting flight to St. Petersburg. It was very disappointing to miss touring the orphanage with Laura Bush, but twenty-two hours of travel with flight delays and multiple connections gave me plenty of time to come to terms with it. There was so much to experience and much work to be done. Now I am looking forward to interviews with the American and international press and to reporting back to ONE members on the ONE blog the news of this G8 Summit.

The boat docks at Strelna, and I follow Meighan and Seth down the pier toward a village of enormous white temporary buildings. They resemble tents. They seem to be made of canvas or vinyl, with large clear plastic windows wrapping all around. As we enter, I hear the air pumps, which apparently are keeping this enormous structure standing.

I enter the largest computer lab I have ever seen or, I suspect, ever *will* see. This open space is easily the size of a football field with hundreds of rows of computers. People and computer wires run everywhere. Aluminum canned lights hang from the ballooned ceiling, and along the perimeter of the building is a row of doors leading to closed-off rooms. Signs hang above each door: Reuters, AP, BBC, NBC, ABC, CNN.

Meighan says, "I need to go receive the recent communiqué from the summit meeting this morning, but stay close. I have an interview for you with NBC. The situation in the Middle East is overshadowing the work of last year's G8 Summit, but this story needs to be told — the world community is sorely behind in keeping their commitments to Africa."

Meighan checks her Blackberry. "I'm not exactly sure when the NBC team is available, so stay close." She bolts out of the building, leaving me alone.

I meander through the aisles of computers and members of the international press. The reporters are focused, typing madly on their laptops. On the computer screens I see Arabic, Italian, German, French, Korean, and characters of a language I have never seen before. I climb stairs that lead to a small second-story lounge that resembles a deck. Instead of the deck overlooking a yard, I stand at the railing, my eyes scanning a room that contains a person from almost every country on the planet.

My life is lived in a homogeneous community. We all tend to talk, look, and think the same. In contrast, this bubble of a building being held up by air is full of members of the global press and the seemingly infinite ideas and opinions of my generation. In this diverse island of languages, ideas, and power, I start to believe in a deeper way. *This can happen.* Never before has a generation had this level of access to one another. Maybe this is our time. Maybe this is our time to come together and make the world a better place for those who are suffering.

Seth hands me a small clip-on microphone, explaining how to hook it on my jacket. I take my seat at a long table. One of the successes of this G8 Summit has been increased commitments to funding the Global Fund to Fight AIDS, TB, and Malaria. As a ONE delegate, I was asked to speak at a press conference for the Global Fund addressing why this funding is significant and why an ordinary American mom traveled halfway across the world to urge world leaders to keep their commitments to the Millennium Development Goals.

Seth begins by responding to a question from a member of the press. "At the end of the 1990s, public health experts identified a number of highly effective ways to prevent and treat AIDS, TB, and malaria. As a world community, a new understanding of epidemics and of the complex causal links with poverty led the United Nations to create the Global Fund. It was established in 2002 with the purpose of fighting AIDS, TB, and malaria.

"Before the creation and success of the Global Fund, lifesaving medication for people living with HIV was priced out of reach for more than 90 percent of those who needed them."

I listen to Seth, nervous for my turn to take questions. He sounds way better than I think I'll sound, but I say a prayer and try to get my thoughts together.

"G8 leaders today affirmed the commitment to end the devastation of HIV/AIDS around the world, joining world leaders in development, economics, public health, nongovernment organizations, the World Health Organization, the World Bank, UNAIDS, and bilateral donors."

Back in 2003, I learned about the Global Fund through my advocacy DGAAN meetings. A delegation of us, including Sister Sheila Kinsey and my friend Brad, met with Henry Hyde, our representative in Congress at the time. The Global Fund was a new entity and was in need of funding from donor nations. Congress was voting on how much money to give to the Global Fund. America is not the only donor; in fact, the Global Fund has many stakeholders, from governments to individuals.

The Global Fund is unique because of its unusual partnership with governments, civil society, and affected communities. It represents a new model of global health financing. For instance, an affected country applies for grants for specific health issues. The Global Fund gives grants to nations in need of funding for HIV/AIDS, TB, and malaria treatment and prevention programs. The Global Fund does not implement programs. Rather, it funds existing efforts. Recipient countries, the nations who receive money from the Global Fund, qualify for the money by having national strategic health plans and priorities, and the Global Fund gives priority to financing nations with low income and a high disease burden.

At the meeting with Representative Hyde, he was surprised by me — the stay-at-home mother from his district lobbying him about the Global Fund. I explained that I cared deeply about the HIV/AIDS global pandemic and that I had never been politically active before learning about the devastating reality of life for mothers, children, and families affected by the pandemic. Where you live, I told him, should not decide whether you live or whether you die.

Seth has finished answering questions. It's now my turn to speak at the press conference. The room is about half full. The tall stadium seating ensures that everyone has a good seat. I nervously observe the pads of paper and the pens frantically taking notes. With a stronger voice than expected, I say, "Fully funding the Global Fund to fight AIDS, TB, and malaria is essential to the well-being of millions of people around the world."

I speak slowly, trying not to jar the microphone clipped to my chest. "As a mother, I would do anything to ensure my children receive needed medical care. Since the creation of the Global Fund, 3.7 million orphans have gotten medical services they otherwise would not have received.

"My mother's heart is comforted by this statistic. I cannot adopt 3.7 million orphans, but as an American and as a member of ONE, I can add my voice to the global community and raise awareness for children suffering in extreme poverty with no one to care for them."

Questions from the press are directed to other members of the panel, and despite trying to keep my mind in the room, I have a mental picture of Thomas as a baby in the pediatric ward of our local hospital. While getting tubes in his ears, he was infected with MIRSA, the super-staph infection that claims lives. It was very scary for a few nights, hoping and praying his little body and the medicines would fight the staph infection and he would be okay. In the end, Thomas pulled through just fine, but that is because he received the medical treatment he needed when he needed it.

I think of Thomas and of other mothers like me who have sat watch over their sick children. The press conference ends and I smile at the room of reporters. "On behalf of caretakers around the world, I would like to thank the G8 leaders for increasing commitments to the Global Fund."

●

I am drunk with exhaustion and experience. The rocking ferryboat is adding to the sensation. Meighan must feel the same, as we are slouched in our seats, leaning affectionately into one another, heads together.

"Well, lady, we did it." She settles into a satisfied sigh.

"You mean you did it. I'm just along for the Meighan Stone Show." I smile playfully.

The ferry is full of tired people, and every seat is taken as members of the press make the final trip back to hotels, taxis, and airplanes.

"Girl, you did some great interviews and wrote some good blog entries for ONE. And that podcast was right on," Meighan says.

We sit for a moment and listen to the hum of the boat's engine and lapping water. I say, "I don't want to sound cheesy, but I respect what you do so much. You are an inspiration to me."

Meighan smiles and wistfully looks out over the dark

water. "Thanks, Shayne. It is very fulfilling. As a woman of faith, I feel honored to have this as my job."

As the ferry approaches the mouth of the river, the lights of St. Petersburg begin to reflect across the small waves.

"Meighan, it's all so inspiring—so hopeful. I had no idea of the role of global public policy and its capacity to reach millions of people in need all over the world. In my faith tradition, we give a lot of money to our churches, missionaries, and ministries who do all this. I am floored by the potential of the world coming together and making real change." I am animated. "I mean, my church is never going to raise $17 billion to help end extreme poverty and AIDS, but as a world community, we can." I am preaching to the choir.

"Yup." Meighan nods and says sleepily, "What if love ruled the world?"

My eyes fill with tears as my heart fills with hope. What if?

- The Global Fund was created in 2002 to raise and distribute resources to fight global AIDS, tuberculosis, and malaria, which together killed over 4.1 million people in 2007.[1]
- The Global Fund has helped deliver 88 million bed nets to protect families from malaria, put more than 2.3 million people on ARV medication, and provided 79 million HIV counseling sessions.[2]
- The Global Fund has become the main source of finance for programs to fight AIDS, tuberculosis, and malaria, with approved funding of $15.6 billion for more than 572 programs in 140 countries.[3]
- Programs supported by the Global Fund have prevented more than 3.5 million deaths.[4]

A MOTHER'S HEART

We cannot all do great things, but we can do small things with great love.

Mother Teresa of Calcutta

Los Angeles, 2008

The jet planes roar over my head as I read my book while simultaneously trying to keep my face toward the sun. At home it is 20 degrees and snowing, but here sitting outside LAX, it is sunny and almost 80 degrees. My starved-for-sunshine body soaks up the weather. I don't care that the smog is so bad I can taste it or that the exhaust from passing cars could choke a horse.

However, I begin to get restless at hour two. I am starting to get hot and I am kind of slimy from the flight and from sitting outside in the heat and grime. I understand Meighan has been filming with Pastor Rick Warren of Saddleback Church in Orange County. Clearly, he takes priority over the Midwestern housewife, but I am getting antsy and ready to move on. I think of going inside, but I do not want to mess anything up for Meighan. She told me to wait here.

Finally, I see Meighan making her way toward me in a silver rental car. I wave and smile, very happy and excited to see her. Meighan is on the phone. I do not interrupt her, but put my carry-on in the backseat and jump in the passenger seat with a silent grin.

Hanging up her Blackberry, Meighan says, "Welcome, lady! I am so sorry that took forever. I totally underestimated how long it would take me to get here from Saddleback. But you look good. It's so nice to see you."

We move out into L.A. traffic. "So are you ready for today?" Meighan asks.

I shrug and smile. "Sure."

"Good. Today you will be filming with Julia Roberts," Meighan says matter-of-factly, with a small smile anticipating my response.

My eyes shoot sideways in her direction. "You are kidding, right?" But I know she is not.

Meighan is producing a PSA, or public service announcement, on behalf of the ONE Campaign. ONE is made up of many high-profile people, but most of ONE's members are just like me, ordinary Americans rallying around the causes of global extreme poverty and disease. Meighan had this great idea for the PSA—to have people standing in a line as if waiting to vote. The line is made up of ONE members outside a voting booth. Some people are easily recognizable public figures in the arts, media, and religion, and others in the line are ordinary people representing the heart of the movement. That's where I come in.

I flew to L.A. knowing I would be filming for the commercial, but, as always with Meighan and ONE, I really didn't know what to expect.

"No way!" I throw my head back, the news hitting me. I start to laugh and shake my head.

In this day and age of advanced media technology, not all the people in the voting line needed to be present to film at the same time. Most people were filmed separately and then edited together. In fact, Meighan had just come from Saddleback Church filming their pastor,

Rick Warren. Today it would be just Julia Roberts and me filming in a studio in L.A.

Meighan is a native New Yorker and works with high-profile people all the time, so to say she is not starstruck is an understatement. I try to contain my giddiness so I don't annoy her, but I am really excited.

Meighan receives a call on her Blackberry, and I look out the windows at the familiar landmarks leaving LAX. It seems like another lifetime when I lived here. I moved immediately after college to teach middle school in the inner city of Los Angeles. I came to L.A. six months after the 1992 riots and lived and worked in South Central. At the time, my school was just blocks from broken windows and burned-out buildings still in need of repair. I was a missionary teacher working for World Impact, an inner-city mission, and I taught at Los Angeles Christian School just off the 10 freeway.

I was young and single and lived with six other female teachers in an old Victorian home, like the many that still line the streets of South Central. I had no car and I had taken a vow of poverty. For two years my life was teaching, hanging out with teens, and living in community with the other missionaries and teachers. I fell into the rhythm of the inner city, and although it was very different from my sleepy Midwestern hometown, I came to have great affection for the place and for the people.

But that was a long time ago. I got married, settled in my hometown, had three babies, and never went back. In fact, this trip to Los Angeles is my first time visiting the city in over a decade. It is surreal to try to juxtapose that time with the present. I have always been missional. I have always had a heart for the poor and the oppressed. I suppose this is not too far off from that time in my life, but instead of heading to minister to marginalized teens, I am heading to a Hollywood studio to play my part in increasing awareness of the world's marginalized people.

But still. It is just so crazy. Julia Roberts?

"This traffic is horrible!" Meighan bemoans. "Here, will you text for me while I try to drive in this?" She tosses her Blackberry to me.

"Ah, okay." Should I tell her I have never held a Blackberry and have no idea how to text?

"Okay, this email is to one of the producers at Oprah." She is nosing the car aggressively into the left lane. "Say: 'That would work. I just need to check out a few more . . .' "

A producer at Oprah? Yikes. Not my usual correspondence. "Whoa, hold on." I try to size up the mini-keyboard in my hands. "Where's T? . . . Okay, I'm getting it," I assure her. "t-h-a-t, how do I make a space? Okay, I got it . . . w-o-u-l . . . where's d?"

"Are you serious?" The traffic and my poor texting skills are getting to her.

I start to laugh uncontrollably. "Meighan, I have never even held a Blackberry before! I'm sorry. It's true. I don't know how to text." I think it is all very hilarious, but then again, I'm not the one trying to produce a commercial with high-profile, busy celebrities. "I'm sorry," I say, trying to pull it together, "I can do it. See, I found d."

"Oh, never mind!" She grabs the Blackberry and proceeds to text one-handed at the speed of light.

The studio looks exactly as it should look according to what I have seen in movies and on TV: a compound of flesh-colored buildings intersected by paved roads. Golf carts dart here and there among the enormous warehouse-size studios.

We enter one of these large warehouses. It is completely empty except for a small set in the very center of the room. I stand and observe as Meighan dives into the action, touching base with the director and the film crew. Someone finally directs me over to the corner of the studio where Wardrobe is set up.

"Um, hi," I say timidly to the tiny brunette Valley Girl apparently in charge of the rack of clothes behind her. "I think I'm supposed to talk to you?"

"Hi, are you in the commercial?" She smiles and sizes me up. Literally.

I am five feet tall and German. Despite my best efforts at working out and avoiding food, I have always been a curvy gal. In the brief time since I entered this alternative reality of Hollywood-studio world, my body image has begun to slide south. Everyone in eyesight is tiny, including the men who are filming or standing around. With each moment in this place, I am feeling my hips get bigger and bigger. It doesn't help that today I am probably the heaviest I have ever been, except for when I was pregnant. In fact, I have never quite lost all that pregnancy weight.

"Yes, I am filming with Julia Roberts when she gets here. I'm a member of the ONE Campaign. I'm a mother from Illinois here to support the movement along with everyone else." Everyone on the set today is working pro bono, or for free.

"Cool!" She nods. "So … what size would you say you are?" she asks, looking at me and then to her rack of clothes.

"I'm probably an eight or a ten." I cringe as I confess the bigger number, knowing I am really the bigger number.

"Ohh," she says with a mock apology on her face, "I don't have anything that big." She holds out the last word for effect.

I laugh outside while feeling completely humiliated inside. "Can I wear what I have on?" I ask. What I have on is what I traveled in: my Frey cowboy boots and some elastic waist, wrinkle-free Cabi gauchos.

"Did you bring anything else?" Clearly my outfit was not going to cut it with her.

"I have my carry-on with a few other things." We go to the wall and I open my bag, displaying the pathetic wardrobe I packed.

In the end, this wardrobe girl, fifteen years my junior, dresses me in jeans, an argyle sweater, and a brown hoodie sweatshirt over the top. I keep looking at her in a curious way as if to say, "Is this how you think Midwestern housewives dress? Too bad you didn't have an enormous pair of overalls on your rack and a piece of hay to stick in my teeth." But I keep my mouth shut and just go with it.

I hang back in the studio, trying to fit in. A grip or a cameraman starts a conversation with me about all the players in the room. Apparently the guy hunched over the monitor is the same guy who did the cinematography for the film *Titanic*. This short, outgoing Californian seems very pleased to be in the same room as all these people and assumes I know who everyone is and that I too am pleased out of my mind. I nod. I smile. I make conversation. And I am pleased, but for very different reasons.

It does not happen very often that people come together pro bono to make a difference for those who are suffering. I take in all the characters in the room, a funny short story all its own, and I feel proud of my generation. Sure, people are here to network, to further their careers maybe, but the end result is a television message about keeping the poorest of the poor in our minds when we vote. Our generation is the first generation on the planet to have such a far-reaching ability to spread messages. At least in this moment, the message coming out of Hollywood is noble.

I begin to hear a murmur, "She's here."

I stand in the shadows and watch as Julia Roberts enters the studio. I am shocked. Not by the nauseating attention immediately suffocating her, nor by her glitz or charisma. I am shocked by how tiny she is. I always had her in my head as a tall, lanky lady, but the woman across the floor from me is my height and I could crush her with my pinky.

There is much fussing over the superstar. She immediately takes control, saying no wardrobe or makeup is necessary, and takes her place on the small set. I hear someone shout, "Where's the soccer mom?"

Taking this as my cue, I say, "I'm right here." And I make my way to stand next to Julia under the lights. I am wishing I had thought to say no makeup and no wardrobe too as I consider having to stand next to this icon of beauty in my frumpy getup.

For a small commercial, there seems to be a lot of arranging of lights, people, this and that. Julia and I are positioned as if we are standing in line to vote. There is a lot of downtime, so we chat. We introduce ourselves.

"Sorry it took so long for me to get here," Julia volunteers. "I needed to feed my babies. Look." She points to some spots on her black top. "Spit up."

I laugh. "I've been there, but my baby is six now."

"How many children do you have?" she asks.

"I have three little darlings. Two boys and one girl." I happily relay their ages and respective grade levels. Then noticing a purse she has slung around her, I say, "I love your bag. My friend got one just like it in Italy recently."

"Yeah, I got this in Italy," Julia responds with a smile. "Best bag ever."

"That's what Juleen says," I say emphatically. "She loves it."

Our chitchatty conversation is interrupted occasionally by the director yelling "Action," at which point we move toward the voting booth. This move involves all of three steps, and to me it seems they have us do this over and over unnecessarily.

I begin to giggle and make fun of this. "Okay, do you think we can get it this time?" I say sarcastically.

Julia laughs. "I don't know. We better stop talking and concentrate."

The whole thing is beginning to feel more like the rehearsals from my high school drama days than an hour in a studio with Julia Roberts. Her phone rings. "Hey, 847 area code, that's near you, right? In Chicago."

I nod. She answers the phone, says a quick hello, and hangs up. "That was my best bud."

"You're not from Chicago originally, are you?" I ask.

Looking surprised that I don't know this, she responds, "No, I'm from Atlanta."

I remember this, but stop just short of saying, "Oh, yeah, I knew that." Because suddenly it seems so strange that I would know such details about someone I just met — and the absurdity of celebrity hits me.

"Hey, I just wanted to say, I think it's wonderful that you and these other high-profile celebrities are lending their support to ONE and to fighting extreme poverty."

"Thanks, Shayne. I am happy to do it. Really." She gestures around at the doting techs, the director, at the set and studio. "It's the least I can do." She smiles at me as the director yells "Action" for the thirtieth time.

The director milks just about everything he can from his time with Julia Roberts before he finally lets us off the set. I slip off into the shadows as the director tries to engage her in dialogue about some party of a mutual friend they were at. Julia looks physically in pain as she tries to be polite, yet at the same time shut down the inane conversation.

I observe her and think, *She's just a mom, like me. She has a mother's heart for the world.* I feel honored to have shared this small space with her.

Julia begins to make her way through the crowd toward the exit, but she turns on her heel and walks straight toward me. A sea of people part and watch to see what she is going to do. It does not occur to me that I am the goal, and I am taken aback when she extends her hand to me and says loudly and with intent, "It was really nice meeting you today."

It may have been my imagination, but I am pretty sure we exchanged a knowing smile. In that moment, it didn't matter that one woman was a superstar and one woman was an ordinary person feeling like a fish out of water. In that moment, it was two mothers who made a sacrifice to be a part of getting an important message out. One woman fed her babies in a frenzy before coming to the studio. One woman left her babies on the other side of the country and was wondering if they got enough protein at breakfast. Both women came together to make sure other mothers and other children around the world might be okay too.

- Across the world, young children and pregnant women are bearing the brunt of poor health systems.[1]
- More than one woman dies every minute from preventable causes in childbirth, and for every woman who dies, as many as thirty others are left with lifelong, debilitating complications.[2]
- Every year, nearly 10 million children around the world die before their fifth birthday, mostly from preventable and treatable causes.[3]
- Almost all maternal mortality (99 percent) occurs in the global South, especially in some of the poorest countries in sub-Saharan Africa.[4]

THE WAY
THE WORLD IS

Many Christians do want to engage the world with their faith but wonder how to do so. They worry about being faithful to the gospel, and about not compromising the church's witness in the world, becoming tainted with partisan politics, or replacing faith with ideology. All these are valid concerns. I believe our faith calls us to transform the world, but how we do so is very important.

Jim Wallis, The Great Awakening

As I continue to wrestle with complex human and political issues, I resolved myself to one thing: the starting point must be that the church is a place where we can grapple with difficult questions with grace and humility. And I believe that, even more important than thinking identically on every issue, we must learn to disagree well.

Shane Claiborne, Jesus for President

My hometown, 2007

I watch the woman get up from her front-row seat and walk quickly to the back of the room where the pastor is sitting. The room is dark and the volume is loud, making it difficult for me to hear exactly what she is saying. She is becoming quite animated, and I watch as the pastor's face clouds over.

It doesn't occur to me that she might be upset by what she is watching.

I turn back to the film *A Closer Walk*. I am presenting a screening of this powerful documentary at one of the local churches near my home. *A Closer Walk* is a film about AIDS in the world, about the way the world is. It depicts humankind's confrontation with the global AIDS epidemic. It follows the stories of people on four continents living with HIV and AIDS. The film profiles a beautiful student in Uganda who was born HIV positive, a family in India struggling with the decision to have children or not within a culture that places this as a high ideal, orphans living in miserable conditions in Haiti, drug users on the streets in Russia, and prostitutes on the streets of St. Louis. All of this is enriched by interviews with caregivers, doctors, social workers, activists, economists, and politicians.

This film may be the best tool to help people unfamiliar with the global HIV/AIDS pandemic explore the underlying causes of AIDS and the relationship between health, dignity, and human rights.

I glance over my shoulder as the woman's animated whispers are distracting. She glares at me accusingly. Did she just point her finger at me? I don't know what is going on. Ignoring her, I turn back to the movie, wishing she would simmer down and return to her seat.

The film ends, and I turn on the classroom's fluorescent lights, hoping to begin a productive discussion. I move to the front of the room and perch on a stool.

The woman is the first to speak. "How can you come here and show us this film?" she demands.

"I know, it is really disturbing—what is happening with AIDS around the globe," I answer in my encouraging ex-schoolteacher tone.

"I cannot *believe* you showed us a film with a pastor passing out condoms on the street. A pastor! I am really offended." She glares at me as if waiting for me to do something about this.

My mind is twisting, trying to follow the logic of my supposed infraction. We have just spent over two hours following the stories of people suffering with HIV and AIDS on four continents.

"I'm sorry. It did not occur to me that would be offensive."

I'm apologizing, hoping to be able to begin a discussion, but my heart is racing with anger that this is all she got from the film. I feel sabotaged. Isn't it obvious that the real issue is global AIDS and what we can do as a community to join the fight?

"How could that not occur to you? Those people are engaging in sinful behavior and they need to stop."

Feeling wildly uncomfortable, I say slowly, "Ah ... we're all sinners, right? I didn't think it would be offensive because it's a film about the tragic effects of global AIDS. People have different opinions on how to fight HIV and AIDS, and some people choose to recommend condoms to halt the spread of the disease so people don't die."

"Abstinence," she pronounces, then looks around as if she expects to get an "amen."

Trying to be diplomatic, I say, "Yes, abstinence is an effective way to stop the spread of HIV and AIDS. However, the reality is some people are going to engage in risky behavior. I mean, just because we would like for them to stop doesn't mean they are going to—and even if we believe their behavior is immoral or irresponsible, does that mean they deserve to die? Does that mean we withhold condoms or other effective measures?"

I continue, unaware of the impact of my words. "Personally, I'm just not comfortable with that."

The room explodes with voices. The pastor leaps to his feet. Clearly, I have overstepped my boundaries here. Everyone is talking at once, and the pastor looks angry.

"Shayne," the pastor says, "I think this topic is a little volatile and we should move on." Then to the room, "I didn't know that was in the film."

●

I throw the DVD of *A Closer Walk* on the front seat of my car. I do not want to accept that my faith tradition is *comfortable* letting "sinners" die. Yet how else am I to understand what just happened? Rather than dealing with the real issue, these people used simplistic morality as an excuse to beat down others who are suffering and dying. I guess if we beat suffering people down far enough, they won't be able to threaten our comfortable lives — maybe we can make them invisible and we won't have to think about them.

If my faith is such an integral part of who I am, how can that faith be used so cruelly? I do not believe everyone in that room felt as strongly as the woman, but why does it seem voices like hers often carry the day? I am fighting tears and cynicism as I drive home. I wonder, *If this is the way the world is, how can the more compassionate voices be heard above the din?*

Thankfully, just a week ago, *A Closer Walk* was better received — although, perhaps tellingly, it was outside the evangelical bubble. With Brad Ogilvie and Sister Sheila Kinsey, I organized and facilitated an advocacy and networking event at the College of DuPage, our local community college. We presented a screening of the documentary film. Display tables were set up in the atrium outside the theater for local organizations and ministries who focus on the AIDS pandemic. People who attended were invited to visit the tables and learn about what is going on locally and globally regarding HIV and AIDS. About 150 people from the community attended the event, including pastors from local Protestant and Catholic churches. It was a time of building relationships within our community, and not one person accosted me regarding condom use.

I admit, I struggle with my church's seemingly paralyzed response to local and global AIDS. Yet I am encouraged this response is not the only one. I am encouraged particularly by Cindy Judge. Cindy is the director of global outreach for Wheaton Bible Church, a conservative Protestant church. When Cindy and her team learned of the devastating reality of global HIV and AIDS, they built their yearly missions conference around it. When the majority of evangelical churches were slow to start or turning a blind eye altogether, Cindy brought this uncomfortable, fraught-with-controversy issue to the forefront of her church. That year they raised a record-breaking amount of money, and it jump-started their AIDS initiative.

Inspired by Cindy, I worked with Wheaton Bible Church. I traveled to Kenya, Africa, as a member of the AIDS Task Force, and I was a founding member of their Heart for AIDS initiative. It was exciting to find other like-minded Christians and to see my faith tradition getting on the bandwagon of support and advocacy.

Partnering with three missionaries in Nakuru, Kenya, along with pastors and health-care workers known as the Nakuru AIDS Initiative (NAI), Wheaton Bible Church has built a strong link to real people in real need. The Nakuru AIDS Initiative focuses on caregivers and on orphans and women widowed by AIDS. In five years of partnering with NAI, Wheaton Bible Church has sponsored five training seminars for hundreds of schoolteachers to use the "Why Wait?" abstinence curriculum for primary and secondary education. They have sponsored seminars and youth camps focusing on advocacy and education around HIV and AIDS.

A few days after the unfortunate screening of *A Closer Walk*, I complain to Cindy over coffee, "It was so discouraging. She took over the whole discussion."

"Shayne, don't worry about it. People hear what they want to hear—what they can handle. It can all seem so overwhelming, like there is nothing we can do, but we have to keep doing what is in front of us." Her words comfort me. "There is hope, even if that woman couldn't see it, and her fear made her focus on the condom issue.

"As Christians, it is important to teach biblical principles when it comes to responsible sexual behavior. But it is not either/or. We need to act out of a place of love and compassion, fighting against stigma and prejudice. The dialogue can be open *and* real healing can take place in communities." Cindy excuses herself to add cream to her coffee.

I reflect to myself that it is not only in Africa where we need to do this. I appreciate the way Cindy partners with Mosaic Initiative and my friend Brad here in town. For the past two years, Cindy and her team have partnered with Brad on a breakfast for the community highlighting the issues of HIV and AIDS globally and locally.

"There are so many things which divide us"—Cindy takes a scone out of a bag—"We are never going to be in solidarity on every issue, but we must be in solidarity over the greater good of fighting global AIDS. And I believe this can be done without compromising who we are or what we believe in." I nod in agreement and Cindy adds, "It may not be ideal, but no one can argue the A approach in African nations has proven effective for preventing the spread of HIV."

The ABC approach stands for "Abstain, Be faithful, and Correct and consistent use of condoms." PEPFAR has supplied 2.2 million condoms worldwide since 2004. These condoms are distributed at Volunteer Counseling and Testing centers (VCTs) in countries receiving PEPFAR resources. Several studies have indicated that counseling for couples, combined with consistent condom use, lowers HIV transmission by 80 percent.

Over coffee, Cindy goes on to remind me of all the hope she finds working in Kenya. She is excited about their Volunteer Counseling and Testing programs, which provide important and otherwise unattainable services to the people who need them the most. Cindy's Heart for AIDS initiative, along with the Nakuru AIDS Initiative (NAI), has sponsored over twenty-five people to be trained as government-licensed counselors for the VCTs. With more trained counselors, more centers were needed, and so they built ten VCT clinics in the communities most in need. Some VCTs are mobile units, enabling the HIV-testing kits and counselors to go into the field to find those who are suffering and undiagnosed.

Our conversation continues far after our coffees are empty. I admire Cindy's approach to partnership because of the respect she has for the Kenyan communities. With a constant ear to the people who live and work in Kenya, Cindy allows programs to respond to needs organically, locally, and from the bottom up. In the past five years, the partnership has provided training for both pastors and lay leaders, sponsoring many people to attend transformational community and health development seminars, home-based care seminars, marriage and general counseling courses, microfinance training, conservation farming courses, and more.

At about the same time I was building a relationship with Cindy and Wheaton Bible Church's AIDS initiative, I also got involved with Upendo Village in Naivasha, Kenya. I learned of Upendo Village at my very first DGAAN community meeting. Upendo Village is a project of the Assumption Sisters in Naivasha, Kenya, and another example of diverse people coming together to make a difference. Because of my work of raising awareness in my hometown, I was asked to sit on the executive board of directors for this fledgling project. This Catholic ministry has several Protestants sit on its board, making it a unique ecumenical experience.

When Upendo Village asked me to be on their board, I was pleased and curious. No one had ever asked me to be on the board for anything before. Despite having a master of arts in theology and a B.A. in communications, I guess no one ever saw me as qualified for such a position, since while I was home with babies my sphere of influence included only my small family and the other ladies at the park. Yet I suggest not-for-profit boards cruise the tot lots looking for prospective board members. Maybe more power meetings should happen at the park. Women connecting with women have real power.

This power is what attracted me to Upendo Village. It

means "village of love" in Kiswahili, and it began as the ultimate grassroots community of women: nuns reaching out to women in need. A handful of nuns working out of a cement room at their local parish in Naivasha, Kenya, began serving the needs of women and children living with HIV and AIDS. The sisters of Upendo Village began by simply feeding those suffering from AIDS who were unable to work or even to get out of bed to feed themselves. Traveling many miles up into the countryside and to neighboring villages, the sisters would bring food and medicine and helping hands. Often after entering a home they would immediately throw open the curtains to let the light in and start doing the dishes.

When I first began to learn about the kinds of programs needed to serve those living in extreme poverty and suffering from HIV and AIDS, it seemed overwhelming: nutrition, microfinance, vocational training, sustainable farming, home-based care, etc. What I figured out is these programs equal one thing: meeting people's basic needs, starting with the most basic need. I have come to respect the work of Upendo Village and the devotion of the nuns in Naivasha. Sister Florence, the director of the health clinic and programs, is well respected and well loved in her community. It is incredibly encouraging and fills me with hope to sit in board meetings and hear the stories of restored health, of education being received, and of families being fed by the services of Upendo Village.

The final image in the film *A Closer Walk* is hard to shake. It is a huge wave cresting and coming straight toward the viewer. It is sobering to picture the AIDS global pandemic this way. AIDS truly is sweeping across the world, cresting in sub-Saharan Africa and washing into Asia, Russia, Europe, and the Americas. It is not a disease that only affects the gay community, or prostitutes, or people engaging in risky sexual behavior, or poor people on the other side of the world. It is destroying mothers and fathers, daughters and sons, future teachers, engineers, philosophers, and artists. I am reminded of what my friend Princess Zulu always says: "AIDS knows no boundaries."

AIDS is a beast hungry to devour us. Standing before it, my voice and influence seem so small against its powerful and unstoppable approach. Sometimes I stare wide-eyed and paralyzed as it rushes toward me. Who am I to fight this?

The wave rushes menacingly toward me, getting louder and stronger, but I do not move — not because I am so brave, but because I am not alone. Despite fear and dread, I stand shoulder-to-shoulder with Brad, and Sister Sheila, with Cindy and her church. There is World Vision and Princess, Sister Florence and Upendo Village, and there are all the members of the ONE Campaign. I stand with world leaders and with Rose as she prays in Honduras.

- Because of its association with behaviors that may be considered socially or morally unacceptable by many people, HIV infection is widely stigmatized.[1]
- People living with HIV are frequently subject to discrimination and human-rights abuses: many have been thrown out of jobs and homes, rejected by family and friends, and some have even been killed.[2]
- Stigma and discrimination constitute the greatest barriers to dealing effectively with the epidemic. They discourage governments from acknowledging and taking action against AIDS. They deter individuals from finding out their HIV status.[3]
- Stigma and discrimination inhibit those who know they are infected from sharing their status, from taking action to protect others, and from seeking treatment and care for themselves.[4]

A NEW KIND OF FULL-TIME MOM

"Then the prophecies of the old songs have turned out to be true, after a fashion!" said Bilbo.

"Of course!" said Gandalf. "And why should not they prove true? Surely you don't disbelieve the prophecies, because you had a hand in bringing them about yourself?

"You don't really suppose, do you, that all your adventures and escapes were managed by mere luck, just for your sole benefit? You are a very fine person, Mr. Baggins, and I am very fond of you; but you are only quite a little fellow in a wide world after all!"

J. R. R. Tolkien, The Hobbit

"Through sacrifice, mercy and charity, women down through church history may have given us our greatest examples of love demonstrated and proven through selfless giving and service to others."

Karen Halvorsen-Schreck, author

Hometown USA, Today

"Shayne!" Mary grabs my arm as I make my way through the crowded party.

"Mary!" I grab back, playfully mimicking her exuberance.

"I have been wanting to talk to you."

I smile and lean against the wall to indicate I'm not going anywhere. Mary and I are attending an annual neighborhood Christmas party. Christmas carols echo through the house, and conversation and laughter are at full tilt. It is a happy night and the rooms are full of familiar faces — high school friends, college buddies, and the many women who made up the community of female support during the precious time when we were having our babies. Most of our kids are school-aged now and life has sped up, leaving these sorts of events as the only time we get to see and catch up with one another.

"Have you read Richard Stearns's book *The Hole in Our Gospel*?" Mary asks passionately.

"Yes, I've read it!" I respond, meeting her enthusiasm. "I thought it was really good."

Mary nods. "I have been meeting with a group of women at my house, and we have been discussing the things he talks about in his book. So we decided to read it together, and we are all so blown away." Mary continues to share why this book and the fight against global injustice, poverty, and disease have her and her friends busting at the seams to get involved. We passionately discuss, agree, and dream as the party merrily continues around us.

Mary confesses, "Shayne, talking with you, meeting with friends, reading these books ... it has put a fire in my heart. I cannot *not* do anything anymore!"

We end our conversation and begin to mingle with the other guests. As I refill my plate of goodies, I can't help but think, *Wow, the difference five years can make,* as I mentally compare my frustrated Christmas cookie exchange moment with the passionate and sincere discussion I just had with Mary.

●

I have come to believe this passion, this heart, this new way to be a full-time mom is a conversation God is having with women all over America. Today I find myself in conversations similar to this one with friends from all over — from San Clemente and Thousand Oaks, California, to New York City and Brooklyn, to Dallas, Texas, and here in my hometown.

The women I talk to want to do more than just write a check. Today women are expressing their broken hearts for the world, a desire to get involved in a meaningful way, and an educated understanding of the issues and complications that come with engaging issues of global need.

We discuss real things, such as throughout the churches of North America, accountability and awareness about global poverty and AIDS are growing. Organizations like

ONE are making it more likely than ever that people will be willing to cross the aisle politically and theologically to work together against these things. In fact, working together is slowly becoming the hallmark of fighting global poverty and disease. NGOs (nongovernment organizations) and NFPs (not-for-profits) and churches no longer work in isolation — that paradigm has been broken. Everyone seems to be partnering, sharing resources, and trading information.

For instance, ONE has over 150 partner organizations; even cities and states, universities and churches are becoming ONE. World Vision and World Bicycle Relief are two not-for-profit organizations that have partnered to bring bicycles to areas of the world hit hard by poverty and HIV/AIDS. These organizations target caregivers — girls and mothers who need to be mobile so they can get to school safely and receive an education, so they can earn a living, care for their families, and pull an entire generation out of poverty.

Enormous entities like the Global Fund are partnering with organizations like DATA and (RED). (RED) was developed by some of the same people who developed ONE. (RED) products engage the private sector, ordinary people, in the fight against AIDS in Africa. (RED) is different in that it is not a charity. It is a business model. When a (RED) product is purchased, proceeds go to support the Global Fund. The Global Fund is supported by donor governments, and it also allows for donations from the private sector. (RED) was designed to kick-start a steady flow of corporate money into the Global Fund. (RED) also sends proceeds directly to Africa, particularly targeting women and children. I recently purchased a (RED) iPod for my daughter, Greta. She is thrilled to have a red Nano with her name etched on the back, and I am thrilled to be able to educate her about the Global Fund and how part of the money from this purchase is helping people in need.

Today I am finding ordinary women like me who care about those who are suffering and who do not wish to hand our children a world in worse condition than when we found it. Women understand there is no easy fix, and we discuss the real disagreements that go on around foreign aid to developing countries. Some want to suggest that aid to impoverished nations, such as the aid from the Global Fund or PEPFAR, is simply a handout and in the long run keeps nations in the cycle of poverty and disease.

However, equating what is going on today in the policy and implementation of foreign assistance with "handouts" is mistaken. Development work requires accountability and transparency and an intense focus on rooting out corruption in governments. Of course, this process is never going to be perfect, but does that mean we stop helping? That we stop providing resources? That approach and mindset will kill millions of people and cause endless suffering.

I remember watching the Kenyan mother walk away from the VCT clinic with her son and her lifesaving medication. Clearly, the Kenyan government has some work to do to root out corruption, but does that mean we turn a blind eye to the suffering of innocent people? Like Jesus, we don't wait for the mess to be cleaned up—we jump into the mess and get to work. We enter the stories of the poor in our midst, and we actively work to bring healing to our world. We learn as much as we can. We are a voice for that mother and for mothers like her everywhere. In many societies, women's lives are not valued as equal to the lives of men. I may not live in those societies, but I live in this world, and I can raise my voice to value a woman's life, no matter where she is born.

I am encouraged as I meet and talk with other "ordinary" women like me, women who can become overwhelmed by the suffering of women and families worldwide, yet refuse to be sidelined by a sense of powerlessness or lack of knowledge. Compassionate women everywhere can throw off any limiting attitudes and engage our families, our churches, and our communities with the story that is playing itself out in the lives of the poor around the world.

What if this conversation God is having with women is just beginning? What if it grows? What if both full-time moms and career women started demanding this focus on our Sunday mornings, at missions festivals, at committee meetings, and at local community gatherings? What if a movement of passionate, educated, and equipped women of faith started to transform how the church and our communities view things like extreme poverty or global and domestic AIDS and its effects on women and families?

Throughout church history, women have been instrumental in reaching out to the needy and marginalized, from the early church, to medieval times, to the women's rights movement, and on up to today. In the 1800s and into the 1900s, there was a movement called the Benevolence Movement. Begun in churches to spread Christianity, it banded women together to work toward abolishing social ills. They worked together against slavery in America, they worked together for temperance reform, and they worked within the trade unions. Groups of women changed social pleas from individual cries into mass action.

It has been said that extreme poverty, relentless debt for countries in the developing world, and preventable disease are our generation's greatest moral dilemmas. They are our slavery, and we must raise our voices in protest.

Nelson Mandela, former president of South Africa, brought a group of eminent global leaders together. They are called the Elders. The Elders offer their collective influence and experience to support peace building, help address major causes of human suffering, and promote the shared interests of humanity. I do not think Nelson Mandela is going to come knocking on my door and personally ask for my help. I am not an eminent global leader, nor do I know any, but I believe as women and mothers of faith we have been underestimating our collective influence when it comes to bringing change to our world.

We women instinctively do things together—in community. What Mary instinctively did with her friends—gathering together to learn, grow, and make a difference—is an idea I also embrace. Wouldn't it be incredibly fulfilling to meet monthly with a group of like-minded friends to learn about our generation's problems that affect other women and then come together to make a real difference. I want to hang out in Juleen's living room with a bunch of friends, with music playing, sipping coffee, noshing on snacks from Trader Joe's—maybe have a glass of wine if we're feeling crazy—and explore together how we want to be engaged. We do life together anyway. Why not set aside once a month to intentionally focus on global justice and on the needs of women and children worldwide?

I see a new kind of global women's movement much bigger than simply raising money for our favorite causes. Today that is only a part of the solution. It is an important part, but I believe what is needed in addition to resources is the mother's heart, the feminine voice on the political and global levels, specifically speaking out against what breaks our hearts in areas ravaged by disease and poverty—things like gender inequality. Women should be able to keep their land when their husband dies instead of the land going to a male family member, making the woman homeless. Women need to speak out against gender-based violence. Women should not be beaten by their husbands as a cultural norm. They should not be raped as a cultural norm. And they should be safe to report such things without retribution.

Mobilizing women is not about separating women and men regarding certain issues. The focus should be on working together—actually working and actually together. This means women working with their churches and communities and with men in positions of leadership. Women working with not-for-profit organizations and engaging on a meaningful level. Women working with political advocacy groups like ONE and having a voice at the policy level. Women speaking on behalf of women in need worldwide with the purpose of working toward the eternal reality of hope for a redeemed and healed world. God has a plan for this world, his creation. It is all going somewhere, and we are called to be his grace and his healing here and now.

Yet around the world, the powerful potential of women too often remains untapped—both here in America, in our churches and in our communities, *and* in the developing world. In much of the world, women make up the majority of people who live in poverty today and are bearing the brunt of extreme poverty and disease. And in many countries, women still lack the most fundamental protections and rights.

We know what is needed to unleash the potential of women and girls around the globe. Interventions to improve maternal health, increased access to education for girls, expanded economic and leadership opportunities—all of these can help women lift themselves, their families, and their communities out of poverty. These investments could transform the future of the world's women and, ultimately, the world itself.

I do not know what will move you or your group of friends, or what will catch your imagination, but here are some tangible things I have done, or still do today, to be involved. Doing these things in community with other women is fun and engaging and creates momentum and real power.

- Become a member of ONE, *www.one.org*. By becoming a member of ONE, you are immediately in the conversation, receiving email alerts, blogs, and "What We're Reading" lists. ONE does the sifting of information and delivers articles and points of action in manageable pieces for the average American.

- Get involved with World Vision and its Women of Vision programs. Sponsor an at-risk girl, and she will get an education through twelfth grade. The single best way to get a nation out of poverty is to educate the girls. Go to World Vision's website and explore the programs and the opportunities for meaningful involvement. Learn how World Vision fights to stop gender-based violence (abuse) and how it fights for gender equality with a goal of empowering both men and women in areas ravaged by poverty and disease.
- Support what your church or denomination is already doing. Meet with your missions director and educate yourself about what your church is doing in areas of the world ravaged by extreme poverty and HIV and AIDS. Share the message and encourage your church and pastors to be globally aware, to join ONE, to be educated about the Millennium Development Goals and the Global Fund. As women and mothers, we can press pastors on their responsibility to educate congregations.
- Buy (RED) products, where proceeds go to support the Global Fund to Fight AIDS, TB, and Malaria. (RED) products can be found at places like Starbucks, Apple, Dell, Converse, Hallmark, American Express, and Gap.
- Sign up for newsletters and action alerts. Most websites of not-for-profit organizations have places to sign up to receive their newsletters and action alerts. For instance, I receive email newsletters from ONE, the

Global Fund, World Vision, Mosaic Initiative, Upendo Village, and Congress. These newsletters keep me informed on new projects, ways to be involved, and upcoming legislation.

- Read books and articles to expand your personal understanding of extreme poverty and global disease and how to combat them effectively. I have compiled a list of some of my favorites on these topics at the back of this book.

- Learn who your Congressional representatives are and write letters to them expressing your concerns. Did you know your representatives keep local office hours and you can make appointments to talk to them in person about what is important to you?

- Join Facebook "causes" pages of your favorite organizations and follow them on Twitter. In this age of online social networks, we have unprecedented ways to receive and share information quickly and effectively.

- Support small indigenous projects. Find organizations that are run by the people for the people. Give of your resources and your time.

- Perhaps you will feel called, or have an opportunity, to serve on a not-for-profit board that serves your local community or a global community.

- Get involved locally with issues of poverty and HIV and AIDS. Get tested for HIV yourself and set an example that everyone should know their status. Help create a community that can modify the experience of being tested—for instance, advocating for home-based HIV testing so that this experience is safe and accessible for all people. Reach out to the HIV/AIDS community around you and encourage your church to do the same.

- Participate in a local HIV/AIDS walk/run, or run in any race or marathon to raise money for your favorite cause.

- With what you have learned, travel to other churches or women's groups and give presentations to educate, inspire, and mobilize other women to get involved.

- With a group of friends or with your Bible study or book club, read *Global Soccer Mom: Changing the World Is Easier Than You Think* and spend time reflecting on your thoughts, stories, and ideas for engagement using the questions at the back of this book.

- Meet monthly with a group of friends and take turns researching not-for-profit organizations, learning about issues of extreme poverty and disease, and report back to your group. Decide together what you wish to support, similar to an investment group where women pick stocks they wish to buy. Some great places to start:

  - *World Vision*—A Christian humanitarian organization dedicated to working with children, families, and their communities worldwide to reach their full potential by tackling the causes of poverty and injustice. There is an exciting project within World Vision. They have developed an educational sponsorship program for at-risk girls in Zambia. By targeting girls and providing an education, even through college, an entire generation will be empowered.

- *World Bicycle Relief*—Provides comprehensive bicycle programs for health care, education, and economic development initiatives to help people survive and then thrive. Compared with walking, the simple, sustainable nature of bicycles empowers individuals, their families, and communities. World Bicycle Relief partners with World Vision.

- *Women ONE2ONE*—A campaign of women working together to have 1 million women put their energy, excitement, and inspiration behind *ONE.org*. Women ONE2ONE is a growing voice made up of people who know that maternal health, girls' education, economic opportunity, and women's empowerment are the keys to fighting poverty and preventable disease for everyone.

- *International Justice Mission*—is a human rights agency that secures justice for victims of slavery, sexual exploitation, and other forms of violent oppression. IJM lawyers, investigators, and aftercare professionals work with local officials to ensure immediate victim rescue and aftercare, to prosecute perpetrators, and to promote functioning public justice systems.

- *Upendo Village*—Has a mission to spread the gospel message of love to women, men, and children who have HIV and AIDS so that they can live with dignity, self-esteem, self-sufficiency, and respect. The members are committed to networking with other agencies in providing health care so that clients can enjoy a free and full life.

- *Growers First*—Empowers leaders in developing countries through free-enterprise coffee programs that directly help the rural poor significantly increase their income through their own efforts. Programs are focused on the ground level grower and on facilitating an overall improvement in their economic and social quality of life. Growers First focuses on economic stability, social enterprise and equity, the environment, education, and health and wellness in communities.

The fight against global poverty and AIDS is *the* fight of our generation. Even though I am a mother living in the heart of suburbia USA, I have come to appreciate my vital role. We are dealing with a complex global situation, and no single method or ideology is going to solve the problems of extreme poverty and disease.

My journey began in my hometown, in my kitchen. It has taken me far away from home and I have experienced some amazing things, but it is a story much bigger than just my experiences and what broke my heart. I believe God is calling all women to enter his story of creative grace and compassion for our generation. It is a story of sharing God's hope and healing in our time.

I am convinced more than ever that real change happens right where we are. It starts with the obedience of a compassionate heart. There is no limit to what our one compassionate voice can do when it is shared with others in making the world a better place. I am only one woman, with one voice, who lives in one town, and goes to one church — but all our "ones" add up. Together we can change the world.

- Investing in women's health, education, and the empowerment of girls is essential to creating healthy families and healthy societies.[1]
- In poor families, girls suffer disproportionately from illnesses such as anemia and from malnutrition. The low status of women, their lack of education, and high levels of sexual violence also mean young women are now the main victims of HIV and AIDS. In sub-Saharan Africa, young females are three times more likely to have HIV than their male counterparts.[2]
- In sub-Saharan Africa, more than 80 percent of farmers are women, yet very few have secure rights to the land they farm. Worldwide, women own just 10 percent of all assets.[3]
- An additional $6 billion a year is needed to be on track to achieve the Millennium Development Goal target and reduce maternal mortality by 75 percent from 1990 levels by 2015.[4]
- In almost every society and in every area, women are breaking down the barriers that have held them and their daughters back for so long.[5]

REFLECTION QUESTIONS

The following questions can be used to spark discussion within a small group or can be used by individuals for personal or journal reflection.

INTRODUCTION: WHO AM I TO MAKE A DIFFERENCE?

1. What is your understanding of the ideas and terms "social justice" and "social advocacy"? Do they hold any negative connotations for you? Why or why not?
2. Are you a busy mother who feels a burden for the suffering of others globally? Do you feel limited in how you might get involved or engaged? If so, describe how you feel, what has broken your heart, and what or who is limiting your engagement.
3. Do you know a good model or guide for how an "ordinary" mom can get involved with issues of global need? Who is this person and what does he or she do? Why do you consider that person to be someone you'd like to follow?
4. What scriptural or historical examples can you think of where others were required to speak and to act on behalf of the powerless, oppressed, and poor? Do you feel we, as a North American church, do this well? Are there

things we are missing? Are we being called to do more? Have women in the church been too passive about the things that truly concern us?

CHAPTER 1: CARETAKERS OF THE WORLD

1. Reflect on the idea that women are the caretakers of the world. As women and mothers, what and who has been given to us to care for? Has this job been overwhelming to you at times? If so, describe situations that have been challenging for you. As caretakers within the church, can we make room in our lives to help women in even more challenging situations?
2. Before reading this chapter, did you know what PEP-FAR is? If so, how did you learn about it? Was it at church? In the news? In conversations?
3. Reflect on the attitudes of the men and women in the class Nettie, the nurse in Kenya, was teaching. How do their responses to Nettie make you feel? Describe your feelings and why this causes a response in you.
4. Think about the old woman clutching her Bible. What do you think the role of Scripture and Bible teaching plays in the fight against global disease, poverty, and injustice?

CHAPTER 2: SHAKING THE FOUNDATION

1. Reflect on the opening quote: "The name of this infinite and inexhaustible depth and ground of all being is God. That depth is what the word God means. And if that word has not much meaning for you, translate it, and

speak of the depths of your life, of the source of your being, of your ultimate concern, of what you take seriously without any reservation.... He who knows about depth knows about God." What do you know about depth, of the source of your being, of your ultimate concern? What do you take seriously without reservation? What do you know of God?

2. Do you believe God talks to people? To you? How? Through preaching and Scripture? Through conversations? Through illness or difficulties? Through prayer or inner promptings? Describe your experiences with hearing God's voice.

3. Are you aware of communities or individuals who care for the sick and poor in your area? Who are they? What do they do? Have you been involved in their work?

4. Have you ever caught yourself in the thought that you wish the poor or homeless weren't in your town or in your neighborhood? Or caught yourself thinking you are thankful they are not? Why do we have these attitudes? What does Scripture have to say about these attitudes, especially coming from people of faith?

CHAPTER 3: VOICES

1. Reflect on the quote by Rabbi Zusya: "When I reach the world to come, God will not ask me why I wasn't more like Moses, He will ask me why I wasn't more like Zusya." What does this say to you? Do you think of yourself as uniquely created with your own gifts, talents, and personal power? If so, describe them. If not, why not?

2. Have you ever been in a situation when people of faith are being overly judgmental, critical, and closed-minded? Have you ever been that person? Why do we do this to one another, especially toward people we love? How can this attitude change within the church? What does Scripture have to say about these attitudes? How can we be generous with one another and spur one another on in good deeds and resist pharisaical attitudes?

3. Reflect on Bono's call to action: "If the church doesn't respond to the plagues of Africa, who will?" What is your understanding of the church in the world? What is the church's role in fighting poverty, disease, and oppression?

4. Reflect on the well-known statistic that in 2002 only 5 percent of evangelical Christians were willing to donate money for global AIDS relief or education. What do you think about that? How does it make you feel? If attitudes within the church have changed since 2002, why do you think the change occurred? Why do you think that attitude existed in the first place?

CHAPTER 4: WHAT IS A NICE SOCCER MOM DOING IN A PLACE LIKE THIS?

1. Reread Arloa Sutter's quote: "Scripture sheds light on the why of poverty by addressing issues of greed, disobedience, isolation, and discrimination, but ultimately the power to overcome poverty and disease lies not so much in assigning blame as in learning to live the Jesus way; to follow him in how he interacted with the poor

and suffering, to take up our cross of loving generosity, kindness, and tenacious advocacy for the poor and oppressed." Arloa is the founder of a Chicago ministry in the poorest part of Chicago. Her expression of living the Jesus way became Breakthrough Urban Ministries. What does living the Jesus way look like in your life? Where do you provide loving generosity, kindness, and tenacious advocacy for the poor and oppressed? Where in your life could you do these things more fully?

2. Have you ever taken a risk and gone outside your comfort zone and tried something new? If so, what was it? Describe your experience. Did it move you toward adding something of value to your life? Was it awkward and humorous? A total disaster? If you are someone who is timid about taking risks, reflect on the reasons for this. What are some tools we could use to help us go outside the box? (For instance, I brought my friend with me to the meeting.)

3. Reflect on the idea of coincidence. Do you believe God directs our paths and reveals people, places, and things to us as guidance to do his will? Should we have an understanding of the difference between coincidence and divine providence? How can we tune in to the things God may be revealing to us?

4. Ignorance can paralyze people. Reflect on a time you were confronted with your own ignorance and lack of understanding. How did you feel? What did you do about it?

Chapter 5: We Don't Know What We're Doing, But We Know We're Doing Something

1. The reality of life for women in other parts of the world can seem overwhelming. Do we sometimes fail to connect with a story such as the life of Princess? Is it easier to shrug these stories off as a faraway problem and claim we have enough troubles of our own here? Do we sometimes not engage in the suffering of others because we do not wish to be disturbed inside and because deep down we feel helpless? What is another option in how to respond?

2. Princess has an intense story and she is not naïve about the hard facts of life. As full-time mothers, and as women in North America, are we too naïve about the reality of life for millions of women and families around the world? Should we know more, learn more, and face hard truths about our world? When faced with the harsh realities of life for others, how can we stay tenderhearted and yet have thick skin?

3. How do you feel when learning about the way women in the developing world are treated and how social attitudes and cultural norms keep women in positions of inferiority and subservience? How do you feel about the idea that how a woman is treated can depend solely on where she happened to be born?

4. What is your understanding of the terms "grassroots social movements" and "community organizer"? These terms are not traditionally used in the church, but in

political, usually liberal, arenas. Do they contain any negative connotations for you? Is it time to claim some of these terms and ideas for the church?

CHAPTER 6: A DIALOGUE LED BY LOVE

1. Reread Ezekiel 16:49: "Now this was the sin of your sister Sodom: She and her daughters were arrogant, overfed and unconcerned; they did not help the poor and needy." Have you ever heard this verse preached when on the topic of Sodom and Gomorrah? If so, describe the teaching. If not, why do you think this is not emphasized?

2. Reflect on the idea that some people in the church would rather be right than be in relationship. What is your experience with this idea? Which should we value more? Do these things need to be mutually exclusive, or can we engage with people who disagree with us in love and respect? Why do you think this has been difficult for the church and for some people of faith? What are your thoughts on the idea that as Christians we ought to learn to disagree well?

3. Do you know anyone who is HIV positive? Are they a friend, family member, or loved one? How has their struggle affected you and changed you? Do you know anyone who is gay? Are they a friend, family member, or loved one? How has this affected you and your attitudes? As individuals, as women, and as a church, can we do a better job of reaching out in love to these communities?

4. Have you ever felt in no-man's-land? Describe your

experience? Did you feel helpless or empowered? Did you do anything to "get out" of no-man's-land, and if so, what? Was it positive (you spoke up about something or accepted differences) or was it negative (you silenced your opinions to simply get along)?

CHAPTER 7: SUDDENLY TOO REAL

1. Have you ever traveled to a poor, undeveloped country? Describe your experience. What were you doing in the country, and did it have a lasting impact on you? Was it a shock to your "Western sensibilities"? On seeing a standard of living so different from the one you are familiar with in the United States, could you relate to feelings of helplessness and anger toward God?

2. After reading about the conditions of millions of people living in slums, what is your reaction? What do we do with the reality that many people worldwide live in conditions worse than the average family pet in America? What are your thoughts on how we can grieve this truth yet engage it with hope?

3. Have you ever had a time in your life when you needed reassurance from God regarding major life questions? Did God show up for you? Describe your situation and how God showed up for you. When you are in situations your heart and mind cannot grasp, do you cry out to God, or do you stuff it, try to categorize it, and deal with it later?

4. At the end of my visit, I pray with Rose. We pray, we cry, we touch. What do you think the role is of these three

things in engaging with that which breaks the heart of God? Explore the idea of shared grace.

CHAPTER 8: JESUS AT THE G8

1. Have you ever been faced with the reality of the perception much of the world has regarding conservative people of faith? Describe your experience. How did it make you feel? How did you handle it?

2. Have you ever felt labeled or limited by your status as full-time mother and as a woman in the church? If so, describe your experience and your reaction to these moments in your life.

3. Isaiah 58:9–10 says, "If you do away with the yoke of oppression, with the pointing finger and the malicious talk, and if you spend yourselves in behalf of the hungry and satisfy the needs of the oppressed, then your light will rise in the darkness, and your night will become like the noonday." Many people outside the church, your faith tradition, or your political party are spending themselves on behalf of the hungry and are satisfying the needs of the oppressed. Why do we sometimes resist these people and these efforts even though we agree with the end result? When it comes to helping those in need, how can we work with people we may disagree with or who do not share a similar faith or even a similar worldview? Do you know examples of this? If so, describe them.

4. Of the eight Millennium Development Goals, is there one that jumps out at you? One that causes your heart

to burn for those in need? If so, which one is it? Can you think of creative ways to engage your community, friends, and church to support it?

CHAPTER 9: A HOPE-SHAPED ACHE

1. This is a difficult chapter dealing with orphans and children in need. As women and mothers, how do these stories affect us? How can we become less naïve about the conditions of children in areas ravaged by disease and poverty, yet not become discouraged to the point of thinking there is nothing that can be done? Is there hope? Why or why not?

2. Do you believe God can or will do something about the plight of millions of struggling children and families worldwide? If so, how do you think he will accomplish this? What are your thoughts on the eschatology (the study of end times and heaven) which was presented in this chapter? Do you feel hopeful for the world? Why or why not?

3. Do you believe God reveals things to people in dreams? Are you a dreamer? If so, describe a dream you have had and its message to you. As a church, why do we tend to undervalue the role of dreams in our spiritual life? In your opinion, should we place more stock or less stock in the messages of dreams? Explain.

4. Reflect on theologian N. T. Wright's quote: "It was a strongly held belief of most first-century Jews, and virtually all early Christians, that history was going somewhere under the guidance of God and that where it was

going was toward God's new world of justice, healing, and hope. The transition from the present world to the new one would be a matter not of the destruction of the present space-time universe but of its radical healing." What is your understanding of where the world is going? Of the world to come? Do you feel God is guiding history, or do you feel we are on our own and he is just watching from above? If he is guiding, how do you see your role in bringing healing to this present world?

CHAPTER 10: WHAT IF LOVE RULED THE WORLD?

1. Are you beginning to have a better understanding of the role of international government policy in the fight against extreme poverty and HIV/AIDS in the developing world? If so, describe your current understanding. In your opinion, why is it important to have a both/and approach — the church must respond and we must also pressure our governments to respond?

2. What are your thoughts on the idea that our generation, because of unprecedented access to one another and to seemingly infinite ideas and opinions, might come together and make the world a better place for those who are suffering? What would it take? Does Scripture offer any insight into this ideal?

3. Describe the Global Fund and how it partners with governments, civil society, and affected communities in the developing world hit hard by poverty and disease.

4. Have you ever gone to visit your congressional representative? If so, what was it about? What was the result? Have you ever written to your representative to express your concerns? Do you believe interacting with politicians brings change? If not, why not?

CHAPTER 11: A MOTHER'S HEART

1. "We cannot all do great things, but we can do small things with great love." Reflect on this quote from Mother Teresa. Does it inspire and calm you? In your opinion, what would be a great thing to do and what would be a small thing? Is there a difference on the impact of healing creation? In your life, what would doing something with great love look like?

2. In the developing world every year, 10 million children die before their fifth birthday, mostly from preventable and treatable causes. Those of us living in the developed world today missed that time in our history before advances in medical treatment and widespread availability of health care. The developing world needs to catch up. What is our role in ensuring this happens? Do you believe it can happen in one generation—that we can be the generation to do it?

3. ONE rallies ordinary Americans and celebrities around the causes of fighting global extreme poverty and HIV and AIDS. Other organizations do similar things. Have you ever visited their websites, become a member, or worked at events collecting signatures? In your opinion, is there value in mobilizing people from every back-

ground, faith, and political leaning in this fight? If so, why and what might be the result?

4. Reflect on the thoughts about Julia Roberts: "She's just a mom, like me. She has a mother's heart for the world." What does "a mother's heart for the world" mean to you?

CHAPTER 12: THE WAY THE WORLD IS

1. Much emphasis has been placed on stigma and discrimination against people with HIV. What do you think about the reality that people are still treated with such disrespect? As women of faith and as a church, what is our role in doing away with stigma and discrimination? In our own communities? In the world?

2. What are your thoughts on the idea that sometimes the church seems to judge and withhold rather than offer love to those who are suffering, especially those with whom we disagree? In your experience, why has this been the case? What keeps the church, and what keeps us from acting in deep compassion?

3. Describe your understanding of what is needed on the ground in places ravaged by extreme poverty and disease. List what is needed and why. Why is it difficult to get these things to suffering people? What do you think is the role of local communities, local governments, faith-based groups, and the international community?

4. Do you attend a church or work with an organization that is involved with issues of global extreme poverty and the HIV/AIDS pandemic? If so, describe

this organization and its programs. How did you get involved? What excited you about it? Is it fulfilling? Have you hit roadblocks in getting others to engage and be involved? If so, what were they and what did you do about them?

CHAPTER 13: A NEW KIND OF FULL-TIME MOM

1. Do you believe God is having a greater conversation with women all over America when it comes to fighting global poverty and disease? Is God speaking to you? Is he laying something on your heart and mind? What is it? Out of the list of ideas of where to begin, what catches your attention and your imagination?

2. Reflect on Karen Halvorsen-Schreck's quote: "Through sacrifice, mercy and charity, women down through church history may have given us our greatest examples of love demonstrated and proven through selfless giving and service to others." Does this match your experience? If so, do you have stories within your family or faith tradition of women being great examples of love, selfless giving, and service to others?

3. Where are you in life? Where are your friends? Do the ideals in this book and chapter resonate with you? Would or do they resonate with your friends? Why or why not? What are your thoughts of the power of the feminine voice in culture, church, and the home? Some believe God is raising up women today to be a voice

for the voiceless globally—a new women's movement.
What are your thoughts on this?

4. Reflect on the opening quote from *The Hobbit*:

> "Then the prophecies of the old songs have turned out to be true, after a fashion!" said Bilbo.
>
> "Of course!" said Gandalf. "And why should not they prove true? Surely you don't disbelieve the prophecies, because you had a hand in bringing them about yourself?
>
> "You don't really suppose, do you, that all your adventures and escapes were managed by mere luck, just for your sole benefit? You are a very fine person, Mr. Baggins, and I am very fond of you; but you are only quite a little fellow in a wide world after all!"
>
> *J. R. R. Tolkien,* The Hobbit

After reading *Global Soccer Mom*, do you have a better understanding of how an "ordinary" mom and woman of faith can get engaged on a global, incarnational, and meaningful level? What is your understanding of your role? Can you see yourself working with God toward the greater reality of healing creation and fulfilling God's purposes in the world? Describe your understanding. Tell your story.

GLOSSARY

advocacy. Speaking up on behalf of another. The act of pleading or arguing in favor of something, such as a cause, idea, or policy; active support.

AIDS. Short for *acquired immune deficiency syndrome*. HIV, in its most advanced stage, becomes AIDS. This is the stage when one's immune system is fatally compromised. It can take ten to fifteen years for an HIV-infected person to develop AIDS; antiretroviral drugs can slow the process even further.

AIDS Foundation of Chicago. The mission of the AIDS Foundation of Chicago is to lead the fight against HIV/AIDS and improve the lives of people affected by the epidemic. Founded in 1985 by community activists and physicians, the AIDS Foundation of Chicago is a local and national leader that collaborates with community organizations to develop and improve HIV/AIDS services; fund and coordinate prevention, care, and advocacy projects; and champion effective and compassionate HIV/AIDS policy.

ARV. Short for *antiretroviral drugs*. These drugs can help slow the progression of the disease and keep full-blown AIDS at bay for years. They help to keep people who are HIV positive alive much longer.

Blood:Water Mission. A grassroots organization that empowers communities to work together against the

HIV/AIDS & water crises in Africa. Use your creativity
to start or join a campaign in your neighborhood.

DATA. Short for *Debt, AIDS, Trade, Africa*. It was created
in 2002 to pressure governments of developed nations
to do their part in the fight against extreme poverty in
Africa. The ONE Campaign grew out of DATA, and
in 2007 ONE and DATA joined together to create a
united global antipoverty organization. In 2008 they
formally merged under the name ONE.

DATA Report. An annual report analyzing the progress of
nations such as the G8 nations in keeping their promises to achieve the Millennium Development Goals.

DGAAN. Short for *DuPage Glocal AIDS Action Network*,
a grassroots advocacy group with the goal of building
a strong AIDS advocate voice in DuPage County, Illinois, and to expand that voice into local, national, and
international arenas.

DOHA. Short for *Doha Development Round* or *Doha
Development Agenda (DDA)*. A round of negotiations
of the World Trade Organization (WTO) to increase
trade between countries by lowering trade barriers
around the world. Current talks started back in 2001.
Congress must approve any proposal before it can take
effect in the U.S.

The Elders. The Elders are an independent group of eminent global leaders, brought together by Nelson Mandela, who offer their collective influence and experience
to support peace building, help address major causes of
human suffering, and promote the shared interests of
humanity.

Franciscan Sisters. The Wheaton Franciscans make up the United States province of the International Congregation of the Franciscan Sisters, Daughters of the Sacred Heart of Jesus and Mary, whose mission is to live the gospel following the spirit of Francis and Clare of Assisi and the group's founder, Mother Clara Pfaender. They work in a wide variety of ministries, especially to aid the poor with health care and housing.

G8. Stands for *Group of Eight* and is made up of the major industrialized nations, including the United States, Canada, France, Germany, Italy, Britain, Japan, and Russia.

G8 Summit. A yearly gathering of the G8 where leaders of the eight countries meet to discuss global trade and economic issues and climate change.

Global Fund to Fight AIDS, TB, and Malaria. The Global Fund is a unique public/private partnership dedicated to attracting and disbursing additional resources to prevent and treat HIV/AIDS, tuberculosis, and malaria. This partnership between governments, the private sector, and affected communities represents a new approach to international health financing.

grassroots. A grassroots movement is one driven by a group of individuals, not a movement orchestrated by traditional power structures. Often, grassroots movements are at the local level, as many volunteers in the community give their time to support a cause.

Growers First. A not-for-profit working in Mexico, Indonesia, Rwanda, and Honduras, resulting in sustainable higher incomes for small farmers, creation of new jobs in the community, and an overall improvement in the social and economic quality of life of the grower and his family.

HIPC. Short for *Heavily Indebted Poor Countries*. The HIPC Initiative is a comprehensive approach to debt reduction, working with the International Monetary Fund and World Bank. Many people and organizations work toward canceling the debt of poor countries.

HIV. Short for *human immunodeficiency virus*. HIV is a retrovirus that infects cells of the human immune system, destroying or impairing their function. In the early stages of infection, the person has no symptoms. However, as the infection progresses, the immune system becomes weaker and the person becomes more susceptible to infections. HIV is transmitted through unprotected sexual intercourse (anal or vaginal), transfusion of contaminated blood, sharing of contaminated needles, and between a mother and her infant during pregnancy, childbirth, and breast-feeding.

IMF. Short for *International Monetary Fund*, an organization of 186 countries. The IMF works to improve monetary cooperation and financial stability among all countries. To reduce poverty around the world and promote sustainable economic growth, the IMF facilitates international trade and promotes high employment.

International Justice Mission (IJM). A not-for-profit working in the developing world, which seeks to make public justice systems work for victims of abuse and oppression who urgently need the protection of the law. IJM investigators, lawyers, and social workers intervene in individual cases of abuse in partnership with state and local authorities.

Jubilee USA. Jubilee USA Network is an alliance of more than eighty religious denominations and faith communities as well as human rights, environmental, labor, and community groups working for cancellation of crushing debt owed by poor countries in an effort to fight poverty and injustice in Asia, Africa, and Latin America.

Live 8. A string of benefit concerts that took place on July 2, 2005, in the G8 countries and in South Africa. They were timed to precede the G8 Conference and Summit held at the Gleneagles Hotel in Auchterarder, Scotland, July 6–8, 2005; they also coincided with the twentieth anniversary of Live Aid. Run in support of the aims of the United Kingdom's Make Poverty History campaign and the Global Call for Action Against Poverty, the concerts were planned to pressure world leaders to drop the debt of the world's poorest nations, increase and improve aid, and negotiate fair trade rules in the interest of poorer countries.

malaria. A disease caused by parasites of the *Plasmodium* genus, which are transmitted to humans via bites of infected female Anopheles mosquitoes. In the human body, the parasites grow and multiply in the liver, then spread to the bloodstream and attack and destroy red blood cells. Each year, the disease kills more than 1 million people, mostly children in sub-Saharan Africa. Key interventions to control malaria include prompt and effective treatment with antimalarial drugs, especially artemisinin-based combination therapies; use of insecticidal nets by people at risk; and indoor spraying with insecticide to control the mosquitoes.

Millennium Development Goals (MDGs). The eight Millennium Development Goals, with a target date of 2015, range from reducing extreme poverty by half to halting the spread of HIV/AIDS and providing universal primary education. These goals form a blueprint agreed to by all the world's countries and all the world's leading development institutions. They have galvanized unprecedented efforts to meet the needs of the world's poorest.

Mosaic Initiative. A grassroots organization whose mission is to end the spread of HIV/AIDS. It is open to anyone and works with both groups and individuals to set goals on preventing the spread of HIV. The partners work closely with treatment and care organizations to insure that people with HIV receive care. The organization also works to overcome the economic and social conditions that contribute to the spread of HIV and other preventable diseases.

Nakuru AIDS Initiative (NAI). A partnership of Wheaton Bible Church with ministers and health-care leaders in Nakuru, Kenya.

NFP. Short for *not-for-profit*. Refers to how organizations are structured.

NGO. Short for *nongovernment organization*. Usually a nonprofit group largely funded by private contributions that operates outside of governmental systems.

In general, NGOs have their own social, political, and environmental concerns.

ONE. A grassroots campaign and advocacy organization backed by more than 2 million people who are committed to the fight against extreme poverty and preventable disease, particularly in Africa. Cofounded by Bono and other campaigners, ONE is nonpartisan and works closely with African policy makers and activists. Originated as The ONE Campaign: The Campaign to Make Poverty History, which merged in 2008 under the name ONE with DATA (Debt, AIDS, Trade, Africa).

PEPFAR. Short for *The United States President's Emergency Plan for AIDS Relief.* PEPFAR is the largest commitment ever by a single nation toward an international health initiative — a comprehensive approach to combat HIV/AIDS around the world. PEPFAR employs the most diverse prevention, treatment, and care strategy in the world, with an emphasis on transparency and accountability for results. The goals of PEPFAR over ten years include support for treatment for 3 million HIV-infected people, support for prevention of 12 million new infections, and support for care for 12 million people infected or affected by HIV/AIDS. Training in HIV/AIDS prevention, treatment, and care will be provided for 140,000 new health-care workers.

(RED). A business model created to raise awareness and money for the Global Fund by teaming up with the world's most iconic brands to produce products with the (RED) brand. A portion of (RED) product sales goes directly to invest in African AIDS programs, with a focus on women and children.

social advocacy. Speaking out on behalf of the concerns of a particular group in society. Such concerns may be rights based or needs based. Social advocates are individuals who will stand for what they believe in for the benefit of the underprivileged, the oppressed, or the disadvantaged. Such advocacy tries to determine what might perpetuate wrong behaviors, policies, or attitudes toward the disadvantaged, the voiceless, and other weaker members of a community.

social justice. The term was coined in the 1840s by Luigi Taparelli, a Jesuit. Social justice is the idea that society should be based on cooperation, not class conflict and competition. The members of society and the church ought to value the sanctity of human life above all else and work toward correcting the structures that perpetuate need.

sub-Saharan Africa. A geographic term used to describe the area of the African continent that is located south of the Sahara Desert. Also those African countries that are fully or partially located south of the Sahara.

tuberculosis (TB). An infectious bacterial disease caused by *Mycobacterium tuberculosis*, which most commonly affects the lungs. It is transmitted from person to person via droplets from the throat and lungs of people with the active respiratory disease.

Upendo Village. A project in Kenya designed to respond at the local level to the needs of women, men, and their children living with HIV/AIDS. The ministry provides resources and support to improve their health, to restore their self-respect, to honor their dignity, and to extend their life so that families are strengthened and can plan for the future. The name Upendo Village means "Village of Love."

VCT. Short for *Volunteer Counseling and Testing Center* for the testing and treatment of HIV. A visit to a VCT usually involves two counseling sessions: one prior to taking the HIV test, known as "pretest counseling," and one following the test when the results are given, often referred to as "posttest counseling." Counseling focuses on the infection (HIV), the disease (AIDS), the test, and positive behavior change. VCT has become popular in many parts of Africa as a way for individuals to learn their HIV status. VCT counselors often use rapid HIV tests that require a drop of blood or some cells from the inside of a person's cheek. The tests are cheap, require minimal training, and provide accurate results in about fifteen minutes.

WHO. Short for *World Health Organization*. WHO is the directing and coordinating authority for health within the United Nations system. It is responsible for providing leadership on global health matters, shaping the health research agenda, setting norms and standards, articulating evidence-based policy options, providing technical support to countries, and monitoring and assessing health trends.

William Penn House. A Quaker program and lodging

center on Capitol Hill in Washington, D.C., that seeks to promote peace and justice so visitors may become greater peacemakers in the world.

Women of Vision. A volunteer ministry of World Vision (a Christian relief and development organization) that equips women to serve impoverished and oppressed women and children worldwide. The ministry seeks to educate and inspire women to action in an effort to alleviate the injustice and inequities that exist for women and their families.

Women ONE2ONE. A campaign of women working together to have 1 million women put their energy, excitement, and inspiration behind ONE.org. Women ONE2ONE is a growing voice made up of people who know that maternal health, girls' education, economic opportunity, and women's empowerment are the keys to fighting poverty and preventable disease for everyone.

World AIDS Day. The World AIDS Campaign is a global coalition of national, regional, and international groups united by a call for governments to honor their AIDS commitments. Its slogan is "Stop AIDS. Keep the Promise." The campaign is governed by a steering committee of global constituency-based networks, with a team of support staff based primarily in Cape Town, South Africa, with others in Amsterdam, the Netherlands. Each year on December 1, campaigners from around the world commemorate the anniversary of World AIDS Day. From conferences to community mobilization, campaigners use World AIDS Day to bring attention to the issue of AIDS leadership on all levels.

World Bank. A source of financial and technical assistance to developing countries around the world. It's not a bank in the common sense, but is made up of two unique development institutions owned by the 186 member countries. At today's World Bank, poverty reduction through an inclusive and sustainable globalization remains the overarching goal.

World Vision. A Christian humanitarian organization dedicated to working with children, families, and their communities worldwide to help them reach their full potential. By tackling the causes of poverty and injustice, World Vision provides hope and assistance to approximately 100 million people in nearly 100 countries. In communities around the world, World Vision joins with local people to find lasting ways to improve the lives of poor children and families.

GO DEEPER: SOME RESOURCES

WEBSITES

EDUCATION AND ADVOCACY

Blood:Water Mission, *www.bloodwatermission.com.*
The Elders, *theelders.org.*
International Justice Mission, *www.imj.org.*
ONE, *www.one.org.*
Women ONE2ONE, *www.one.org/women.*
World Vision's Advocate Network, *www.seekjustice.org.*

ORGANIZATIONS TO GET INVOLVED

Growers First, *www.growersfirst.org.*
Mosaic Initiative, *www.mosaicinitiative.org.*
(RED), *www.joinred.org.*
Upendo Village, *www.upendovillage.org.*
Women of Vision, *www.worldvision.org/content.nsf/
getinvolved/women-of-vision-home.*
World Bicycle Relief, *www.worldbicyclerelief.org.*

GLOBAL ENTITIES AND GLOBAL POLICY

Congress and Roll Call (the newspaper of Capitol
Hill), *www.congress.org.*

DATA Report, *www.one.org/international/ datareport2009*.

The Global Fund to Fight AIDS, TB, and Malaria, *www.theglobalfund.org*.

PEPFAR, *www.pepfar.gov*.

USAID, *www.usaid.gov*.

BOOKS

EDUCATION AND ADVOCACY

The aWake Project: Uniting Against the African AIDS Crisis by sixteen contributors, including Nelson Mandela and Bono.

The End of Poverty: Economic Possibilities for Our Time by Jeffrey D. Sachs.

God's Politics: A New Vision for Faith and Politics in America by Jim Wallis.

Half the Sky: Turning Oppression into Opportunity for Women Worldwide by Nicholas D. Kristof and Sheryl WuDunn.

Warrior Princess: Fighting for Life with Courage and Hope by Princess Kasune Zulu.

FAITH AND CHURCH

Compassion: A Reflection on the Christian Life by Henri J. M. Nouwen, Donald P. McNeill, and Douglas A. Morrison.

The Divine Conspiracy: Rediscovering Our Hidden Life in God by Dallas Willard.

Embracing Your Second Calling: Finding Passion and

Purpose for the Rest of Your Life by Dale Hanson Bourke.

The Hole in Our Gospel: What Does God Expect of Us? The Answer That Changed My Life and Might Just Change the World by Richard Stearns.

Love Is an Orientation: Elevating the Conversation with the Gay Community by Andrew Marin.

Jesus for President: Politics for Ordinary Radicals by Shane Claiborne and Chris Haw.

She Did What She Could: Five Words of Jesus That Will Change Your Life by Elisa Morgan.

Surprised by Hope: Rethinking Heaven, the Resurrection, and the Mission of the Church by N. T. Wright.

ACKNOWLEDGMENTS

I gratefully acknowledge the following people:

Andrew Bronson — whose original enthusiasm for this book to be written was instrumental in making it a reality.

Meighan Stone — the lovely lady who first gave encouragement and opportunity to use my voice — for being an inspiration to me as a woman in the world.

Linda Richardson — my spiritual director — for prayerful, loving guidance toward this book.

Sister Sheila Kinsey — a true light in the world — for being my first mentor and guide on all things global social justice.

Juleen Ritchie — whose companionship is treasured beyond measure — for journeying with me so purely and so consistently.

Jennifer Grant — my friend who encouraged me with ideas, conversations, edits, and who coined the term, "Global Soccer Mom."

The Thread — my cyber community, the place where I took off the training wheels on my written voice — for being a place where iron sharpens iron, and for all the humor, grace, and gratitude among friends.

Redbud Writers Guild — my writers group — for friendship and support as we fearlessly seek to expand the feminine voice in our churches, communities, and culture. *www.redbudwritersguild.com*

Angela Scheff—my editor, whose encouragement and patience with this first-time author was immensely supportive and empowering.

Dotty and Dave Klopfenstein—my mom and dad—for supporting me with child care, manuscript suggestions, and a lifetime of guidance.

Johnny Moore—my husband—for making room in our lives for this project, for cheering for me, and for loving me no matter how loud my voice gets.

NOTES

CHAPTER 1: CARETAKERS OF THE WORLD

1. 2009 PEPFAR Annual Report, *www.pepfar.gov/press/fifth_annual_report/*.
2. 2009 PEPFAR Annual Report, *www.pepfar.gov/press/fifth_annual_report/*.
3. *www.joinred.org*.
4. *www.joinred.org*.

CHAPTER 3: VOICES

1. Barna, *www.christianitytoday.com/ct/2005/january/8.22.html*.
2. *www.one.org*.
3. *www.one.org*.
4. *www.one.org*.
5. *www.one.org*.
6. *www.one.org*.

CHAPTER 4: WHAT IS A NICE SOCCER MOM DOING IN A PLACE LIKE THIS?

1. *en.wikipedia.org/wiki/advocacy*.
2. *www.one.org*.
3. *www.one.org*.

CHAPTER 5: WE DON'T KNOW WHAT WE'RE DOING, BUT WE KNOW WE'RE DOING SOMETHING

1. *theelders.org/womens-initiatives.*
2. *www.thebody.com/content/world/art51703.html.*
3. *www.unicef.org.*

CHAPTER 6: A DIALOGUE LED BY LOVE

1. *www.cdc.gov/HIV/topics/surveillance/resources/factsheets/ incidence.htm.*
2. *www.cdc.gov/HIV/topics/surveillance/resources/factsheets/ incidence.htm.*
3. *www.cdc.gov/HIV/topics/surveillance/resources/factsheets/ incidence.htm.*

CHAPTER 7: SUDDENLY TOO REAL

1. *www.one.org.*
2. *www.one.org.*
3. *www.one.org.*

CHAPTER 8: JESUS AT THE G8

1. This title is from an article by Tony Carnes, *www.christianitytoday.com/ct/2005/julyweb-only/33.0.html.*
2. ONE has become a global organization with offices in London, Berlin, Nigeria, Brussels, and Washington, D.C. It has activities in many countries.
3. *www.imf.org/external/pubs/ft/survey/so/2007/new0720a. htm; www.worldbank.org/html/extdr/mdgassessment.pdf.*

4. *www.one.org.*

5. *www.one.org.*

6. *www.one.org.*

7. *www.one.org.*

8. *www.one.org.*

9. *www.one.org.*

10. *www.one.org.*

CHAPTER 9: A HOPE-SHAPED ACHE

1. N. T. Wright, *Surprised by Hope: Rethinking Heaven, the Resurrection, and the Mission of the Church* (New York: HarperOne, 2008), 210.

2. *www.one.org.*

3. *www.one.org.*

4. *www.one.org.*

CHAPTER 10: WHAT IF LOVE RULED THE WORLD?

1. *www.theglobalfund.org.*

2. *www.theglobalfund.org.*

3. *www.theglobalfund.org.*

4. *www.joinred.org.*

CHAPTER 11: A MOTHER'S HEART

1. *www.one.org.*

2. *theelders.org/media/news/lets-stop-womens-suffering.*

3. *www.one.org.*

4. *theelders.org/media/news/lets-stop-womens-suffering.*

CHAPTER 12: THE WAY THE WORLD IS

1. *www.unaids.org.*
2. *www.unaids.org.*
3. *www.unaids.org.*
4. *www.unaids.org.*

CHAPTER 13: A NEW KIND OF FULL-TIME MOM

1. *theelders.org/womens-initiatives/health-care.*
2. *theelders.org/womens-initiatives/health-care.*
3. *theelders.org/womens-initiatives/property-and-inheritance-rights.*
4. *theelders.org/media/news/lets-stop-womens-suffering.*
5. *theelders.org/womens-initiatives.*

World Vision®

Building a better world for children

womenofvision.wordpress.com/

Women of Vision is a volunteer ministry of World Vision, a Christian relief and development organization, which equips women to serve impoverished and oppressed women and children worldwide. We seek to educate and inspire women to action in an effort to alleviate the injustice and inequities that exist for women and their families.

www.one.org

ONE is a grassroots campaign and advocacy organization backed by more than 2 million people who are committed to the fight against extreme poverty and preventable disease, particularly in Africa. Cofounded by Bono and other campaigners, ONE is nonpartisan and works closely with African policy makers and activists.

ONE achieves change through advocacy. We hold world leaders to account for the commitments they've made to fight extreme poverty, and we campaign for better development policies, more effective aid, and trade reform. We also support greater democracy, accountability, and transparency to ensure policies to beat poverty are implemented effectively.

GROWERS FIRST

www.GrowersFirst.org

Growers First builds life changing partnerships with the world's agricultural poor. By helping strengthen or build local cooperatives and grow successful farming enterprises, Growers First empowers families to make their own way out of poverty through hard work and entrepreneurial ingenuity. Growers First works with emerging local community leaders to identify needs and mobilize resources to address long-term socio-economic and environmental challenges. The result is true and lasting community transformation — *a place at the table for the world's poor.*

Real transformation. Real traceability. True sustainability.

www.worldbicyclerelief.org

People in developing nations suffer every day due to lack of transportation: people without access to health care die of treatable diseases and injuries; people without access to education and economic opportunities live in poverty. Bicycles are simple, sustainable and appropriate technology to support people in developing nations and to aid in disaster recovery. The mission of World Bicycle Relief is to provide access to independence and livelihood through The Power of Bicycles. Please visit us at www.worldbicyclerelief.org to learn more about our work.

Share Your Thoughts

With the Author: Your comments will be forwarded to the author when you send them to *zauthor@zondervan.com*.

With Zondervan: Submit your review of this book by writing to *zreview@zondervan.com*.

Free Online Resources at
www.zondervan.com

Zondervan AuthorTracker: Be notified whenever your favorite authors publish new books, go on tour, or post an update about what's happening in their lives at www.zondervan.com/authortracker.

Daily Bible Verses and Devotions: Enrich your life with daily Bible verses or devotions that help you start every morning focused on God. Visit www.zondervan.com/newsletters.

Free Email Publications: Sign up for newsletters on Christian living, academic resources, church ministry, fiction, children's resources, and more. Visit www.zondervan.com/newsletters.

Zondervan Bible Search: Find and compare Bible passages in a variety of translations at www.zondervanbiblesearch.com.

Other Benefits: Register yourself to receive online benefits like coupons and special offers, or to participate in research.

◢ ZONDERVAN®

ZONDERVAN.com/
AUTHORTRACKER
follow your favorite authors